G000054320

Praise for **Leadershi**

'A fascinating and highly readable account of leadership, in all its forms, from one of the most perceptive observers on the scene today.'

Paul Polman, CEO, Unilever

'Anyone imagining that business news stories date quickly should read this book. A treasure trove of great business stories coupled with exquisite, practical insight, it is essential for any business leader seeking to stay challenged and up to date. A lifetime's sceptical inquiry gives Andrew Hill a clear view into the critical sources of business success and failure.'

Margaret Heffernan, CEO and author, *Wilful Blindness*

'Who better than Andrew Hill to insightfully guide us through the important lessons of the "8 acts of leadership." Skilfully analysing both current and historical cases, he provides a refreshing take on leadership in an age of rapidly changing pressures on companies, where preserving competitive advantage is undermined by "fluctuating competition, short-lived opportunities and constant challenge." The result is a perceptive and engaging book that helps leaders transition from "default management" to empowering and enabling their managers to be as effective as they can and should be.'

Mohamed A. El-Erian, author, *When Markets Collide* and *The Only Game in Town*

'An acute and insightful observer of corporate leadership, in this book Andrew Hill delights and intrigues. Full of wisdom and with touches of deep humour, it is a must read for anyone who wants to learn more about what it takes to lead at the top.'

Lynda Gratton, Professor of Management Practice, London Business School

'Andrew Hill's excellent book is not just an essential tour of today's most heated management debates, it's also a robust framework for anyone looking to lead more effectively. His powerful mix of headline news, cutting-edge research and plain-spoken language makes it essential reading for anyone asking the perennial question: "What do leaders really do?"'.

Herminia Ibarra, The Cora Chaired Professor of Leadership and Learning, INSEAD

'I read this in one go! It captures beautifully the "pipework and poetry" of corporate leadership with careful analysis, wit and intelligent advice for the immense personal challenge it offers.'

Dame Clara Furse DBE, Chief Executive of the London Stock Exchange, 2001–9

'Andrew Hill's success in this book lies in his ability to understand both the human dimension of leadership based on years of experience of grilling CEO's and, at the same time, dispassionately analyse the underlying reality beneath the corporate spin. A compelling read with lessons for all of us.'

Sir Ian Cheshire, Lead Non-Executive Director for the UK Government and former CEO, Kingfisher plc

Leadership in the headlines

PEARSON

At Pearson, we believe in learning – all kinds of learning for all kinds of people. Whether it's at home, in the classroom or in the workplace, learning is the key to improving our life chances.

That's why we're working with leading authors to bring you the latest thinking and best practices, so you can get better at the things that are important to you. You can learn on the page or on the move, and with content that's always crafted to help you understand quickly and apply what you've learned.

If you want to upgrade your personal skills or accelerate your career, become a more effective leader or more powerful communicator, discover new opportunities or simply find more inspiration, we can help you make progress in your work and life.

Every day our work helps learning flourish, and wherever learning flourishes, so do people.

To learn more, please visit us at **www.pearson.com/uk**

The Financial Times

With a worldwide network of highly respected journalists, *The Financial Times* provides global business news, insightful opinion and expert analysis of business, finance and politics. With over 500 journalists reporting from 50 countries worldwide, our in-depth coverage of international news is objectively reported and analysed from an independent, global perspective.

To find out more, visit **www.ft.com**

Contents

Foreword

The many admirers of Andrew Hill's columns in the *Financial Times* will be delighted to find that a selection of these columns has been resurrected in this book. It is no longer true that today's newspaper is tomorrow cast into the fire, given that you will still find its contents reserved somewhere in the interstices of cyberspace. In theory, therefore, you can continue to read news and comments from years back, if, that is, you know what you are looking for and where to find it. The reality is that, as we hurry through our lives, what we failed to read today we will never see again. We should be thankful, therefore, that books still exist and can often act as treasuries of the words of the past.

This particular treasury focuses on leadership. It won't be the first book on the subject nor the last because, as Andrew points out, all leaders are now in the headlines, not always for the reasons they would like. Endlessly fascinating though the topic is, it remains elusively hard to define. Many have tried, and Andrew quotes many of them, but good leadership is like beauty, you know it when you see it, but because of its almost infinite variety and its varied contexts and personalities, it defies any precise definition. That is why this book succeeds where many fail, because Andrew shows us some of that variety and lets each example speak for itself, with its flaws as well as its merits. Just as beauty lies in the eye of the beholder, so we may each choose which example or aspect of leadership best fits us in our particular situation.

As guide to the leadership scene, Andrew could not be bettered. The FT brand, as he says, opens most doors, and he has put his foot in many of the most fascinating. Well-read (indeed I am amazed by his coverage of the ever-expanding literature on this subject) and well-travelled (for he has covered much of the world and, exhaustively, many of its conferences), his columns allow us to be voyeurs of the lives and words of more people, and more interesting people, than most of us would ever get to meet.

Realising that an undiluted series of his columns might be a little indigestible, Andrew has divided them up into nine chapters, with titles that in themselves provide a guide to the key aspects of leadership, from planning, moving and making to coping, sharing and, not least, leaving, as well as a final selection on leading in the 21st century. He provides a linking commentary and, usefully, summarises his own conclusions at the end of each section.

As his readers already know, Andrew's columns are always readable as well as instructive. This, then, is a book that every leader or would-be leader should keep by their side, to use for refreshment, enlightenment and, occasionally, for warning; for leadership is not something to be taken on light-heartedly or vaingloriously but as a big responsibility in these changing times. I thought that I knew a lot about this topic - until I read this book, when I realised how much there was that I didn't know. Others may well feel the same.

Charles Handy
Writer and social philosopher
London

Acknowledgements

Columns usually appear under one byline and purport to be the work of one author. But I would have found it impossible to produce the articles that are the backbone of this book without the advice, knowledge and feedback generously and uncomplainingly supplied by colleagues at the *Financial Times*.

Ravi Mattu and Adam Jones, successive editors of the FT's Business Life pages, and Harriet Arnold, their deputy, worked on many of the weekly columns when they first appeared. They have been, and remain, patient sounding boards for my ideas. While I take responsibility for everything that appears under my name, they and many other editorial colleagues have saved me from bad calls and occasionally from outright errors.

Nicole Eggleton at Pearson Education first planted the idea of a book that would collect some of my columns in one place, and her colleague David Crosby offered useful advice and brought the manuscript to life. At the FT, I am grateful to James Lamont and Leyla Boulton for helping to sort out the copyright and legal niceties required to republish the original articles and for smoothing the way for this novel joint venture.

I am well aware that without the FT's support and the power of the FT brand, fewer leaders would have opened their door to me, but I remain grateful to the business people, academics and advisers who have over the years offered me so many insights into leadership and management. Above all, thank you to my family – my wife Jimena, and our children Tomás and Ana, and my mother

Judy and brother Jeremy – for their continued love, support and good humour.

Publisher's acknowledgement

All *Financial Times* articles © The Financial Times Limited. All Rights Reserved.

sure the toilets work and that there is somebody to answer the telephone'. But he adds that leaders also need the gifts of a poet, 'to find meaning in action and render life attractive'.

Poetry is the last thing on leaders' minds, as they engage in the humdrum daily effort of keeping their organisation afloat, their teams motivated, and their profit margins fat. When Lou Gerstner said in 1993 that 'the last thing IBM needs right now is a vision', he was making clear that the priority at that point was the computer group's plumbing, not its poetry.

Vision has its place, though, even if, in a world where much of the high-profile work at companies is conducted in the headlines, it may seem dangerous to make lofty declarations about purpose and values. The recent shaming of Stephen Green (now Lord Green), former chairman of HSBC, who laid out his principles on money and morality in a 2009 book, *Good Value*, only to suffer charges of hypocrisy when various scandals at the bank came to light, is a good cautionary tale. But criticism – or the fear of it – should not deter leaders from trying to ensure that their organisations do the right thing, or from framing their objectives in ambitious terms. Prof March was not suggesting that chief executives should only be interested in poetry, let alone be able to encapsulate their strategy in language worthy of Shakespeare or Cervantes. He instead hit on the truth that if you neglect either the pipework or the poetry of leadership – or concentrate on one but not both – your organisation is likely to wither.

I do not share the conviction of some radical management thinkers that technology, transparency and generational shifts will instantly change everything for leaders and managers. Unfortunately, old corporate structures and hierarchies have a built-in inertia. At the same time, more positively, some established leadership practices – not to mention the structures of traditional management that make breakthroughs possible and affordable – are still valuable.

But I am convinced that leaders need constantly to refresh and renew the way they run their organisations, to keep up with the rapidly changing pressures on companies, and to try to stay ahead of the headlines. As Whole Foods' Mr Mackey suggested, it comes with the territory to be hailed as a visionary one day, and condemned as a village idiot the next. But as I explained in this column from November 2014 why leaders who continued to do the same things, in the same way, with the same people, were bound to fail.

The default mode for managers needs a reset

By Andrew Hill

Financial Times November 10, 2014

Grayson Perry, the transvestite artist, took aim last month at 'default man':[3] the cabal of white, middle-class, heterosexual, middle-aged males who run the British establishment.

His acid article touched on the cohort's domination of boardrooms. But I think there is a group that has a more insidious influence on modern business: default managers.

Default managers are still, mostly, men. But it is not their gender, but the agenda they follow that often prevents businesses improving and innovating. They are holding back the 'great transformation' of management that academics, executives, entrepreneurs and commentators will discuss at this week's Global Peter Drucker Forum in Vienna. The premise of the conference, which commemorates the work of the late management thinker, is that such change is essential to restore growth and prosperity.

Default managers fit easily into a recognisable and established corporate hierarchy, run on a basis of old-fashioned command and control and governed by title and status. They are usually passive, carrying out instructions that are either explicit in orders from the top or implicit in budgets, accounting timetables, and short-term targets and incentive plans.

Default managers prefer to stay within divisional silos, suspicious of ideas that are 'not invented here'. They may as a result become detached from the purpose, and even values, of their company. Employers, meanwhile, find it easier to treat them as 'collections of human resources' rather than 'communities of human beings', to cite a powerful pamphlet on 'Rebalancing Society'[4] by Henry Mintzberg, the management expert.

I do not blame people who squeeze themselves into this template of default management. It is the destiny of many of those who fight for promotion. They work hard, have good intentions, and may have no ambition to change the framework they inhabit. Revolution, even achieved peacefully, takes time and effort and puts at risk predictable, comfortable routines. But as Prof Mintzberg points out, east Europeans were able to bring about the collapse of communist regimes 25 years ago in part because they always 'understood full well how enslaved they were by their system of governance'. Many default managers, by contrast, have lost sight of the fact that they are cogs in a misfiring machine. More worryingly, they fail to recognise they have the potential to change it.

As Herminia Ibarra wrote,[5] the alternative is not to install in their place a new set of flamboyant, revolutionary leaders. Organisations will continue to need people who can run them efficiently and well. Those managers will always include a few who are inert or merely reactive.

So the priority is not to tear down the organisations themselves, but to remove the largest obstacles that are preventing good managers from becoming more active, more engaged, more collaborative, more open, and more far-sighted. The barriers include monetary incentives that are over-detailed and geared towards short-term performance. Shareholder-owned companies are in thrall to institutional investors, motivated by similar bonus plans based on even shorter timescales. Old corporate hierarchies assign importance to people with the correct title, rather than those who exercise the right skills or greatest influence. They are geared to owners' demands more than to customers' needs. Too often, recruiters seem to be driven by the old catchphrase that 'nobody ever got fired for buying IBM', the default personal computer system.

Lack of public trust in business generally, and managers specifically, is a final problem. Since 2008, many defenders of shareholder capitalism have analysed the causes of the financial crisis and ended up paraphrasing Winston Churchill's comment on democracy and arguing that it is the worst form of economic system apart from all the others. That is too easy a conclusion.

But it is also facile to presume that all managers are part of the problem – a view heard depressingly often, even from people working within business. As Julia Kirby and Richard Straub wrote, launching **an online debate**[6] ahead of this week's Drucker Forum: 'If managers have the power to drive an economy into a ditch, they also have the power to drive it forward.'

But if businesses continue to put default managers in the driving seat, they will never reach their destination.[7]

Source: Hill, A. (2014) The default mode for managers needs a reset, *Financial Times*, 10 November 2014.
© The Financial Times Limited 2014. All Rights Reserved.

A note on structure and terminology

This book groups a selection of my *Financial Times* columns from 2011 to 2015 into sections – eight 'acts' of leadership. I have used simple, two-syllable descriptions – planning, moving, making, shaping, growing, coping, sharing and leaving – rather than the more familiar, but sometimes misleading and overused, terms of art, such as 'strategy' and 'innovation'. In the final chapter – 'Leading in the 21st century' – I have tried to look forward to suggest what will influence future leaders and what challenges they will face.

I generally use the descriptions 'executive', 'manager' and 'leader' interchangeably, because I have found that the best leaders are those who fulfil all three roles. These people are able to describe what they do in relatively simple terms, using practical examples, and concentrating on the real outcomes for their organisations, customers, staff and shareholders.

Herminia Ibarra of Insead has written that 'management entails doing today's work as efficiently and competently as possible within established goals, procedures and organisational structures', whereas leadership 'is aimed at creating change in what we do and how we do it'.[8] It is a good distinction. But I also take heed of what Henry Mintzberg has proposed: 'an end to the belief that leadership is separate from management, and superior to it'. 'Have you ever been managed by someone who didn't lead?' he wrote in 2015. 'That must have been awfully discouraging. Well, how about being lead by someone who didn't manage? That could have been much worse. How is such a "leader" to know what's going on?'[9]

Planning

Planning ought to be the fundamental first act of any leader. 'What is your plan?' is the question that nags at new chief executives, project managers or divisional heads.

It is why many chief executives start by conducting a strategy review. Take stock, ask questions of your team, and of your team's team, look again at the plans of your predecessor. These seem sensible ways to approach a new role. After all, if you are replacing someone who has not lived up to expectations – or even someone who has – the old strategy may need refreshing.

The problem is that the ground shifts under a new CEO's feet even as she maps out her first weeks in charge. The days are long gone when an executive team could prepare a five-year plan, execute it and then expect to enjoy the fruits of competitive advantage until the time came to write the next one.

I remember being impressed by the strategy review that Samir Brikho conducted when he took over as chief executive of Amec, the engineering services group, in 2006. Seventy-five days later, he presented to analysts not a wish list, but a plan that was already well under way. His presentation included a brutal reminder of the complex organigram of 54 senior executives he had inherited. 'Who is responsible for what? Who is accountable for what? It constrains growth, it inhibits decision-making and there's a big space for internal politics,' he pointed out. Not many survived.

A second difficulty is that few chief executives, even those who pay lip service to the idea of strategy, truly understand the concept.

One of the first business academics I met after I became the *Financial Times* Management Editor in 2011 was Richard Rumelt, an irascible strategy expert, who was on tour promoting – I thought a little reluctantly – an excellent book, based on a lifetime's experience debunking received wisdom about strategy and planning. I wrote this column mingling his insights with the concerns executives raise about the difficulty of setting a course for their businesses.

Strategies founder on fluff and buzzwords

By Andrew Hill

Financial Times June 13, 2011

Few terms of corporate art are more abused than strategy and its cousins. Put 'strategic' ahead of simple decisions (strategic acquisition, strategic initiative, strategic hiring) and the people carrying them out can feel more important, while those advising can charge a higher fee.

Since January, the FT has reported that more than 30 organisations – from Abertis, the Spanish airports operator, to Zenergy Power, the superconductor developer – are carrying out, will carry out or have carried out some sort of strategy review. In principle, this should be a good thing. In the face of clear evidence of the dangers of complacency or inertia (Blockbuster ambushed by Netflix; Nokia surprised by Apple), all companies ought to revisit more frequently the threats they face and what they must do to neutralise them. The act of reviewing strategy should at least lead over time to improvements in making and pursuing it, shouldn't it?

Not so. In 216 BC, Hannibal, dubbed the father of strategy, beat a larger Roman army at Cannae with what has become a classic military outflanking manoeuvre. Yet, 22 centuries later, says Richard Rumelt of UCLA, organisations have not really built on the superiority established by the Carthaginians. Far from having evolved to a higher level of strategic thinking, most leaders are still winging it and, as he drily points out in his new book, *Good Strategy/Bad Strategy*, 'winging it is not a strategy'.

Despite Prof Rumelt's lofty reputation in this crowded field, *Good Strategy/Bad Strategy* is his first book aimed at a general audience and only his second as a sole author since 1974. While he has vented about strategy in articles, in lectures and in advisory work for companies, he has bottled up plenty of frustration over the past decades. As he explained to me last week: 'Most of the world isn't intending to get [strategy] wrong: they aren't getting it at all.'

In fact, it is worse than that. Many companies are actively pursuing bad strategies. A bad strategy is not the same as a strategy that founders because of miscalculations or mistaken choices (I suspect Prof Rumelt has a soft spot for these decisive failures) but it is the antithesis of good strategy. It's all too familiar hallmarks are: fluff: a 'superficial restatement of the obvious combined with a generous sprinkling of buzz-words'; failure to face the problem; mistaking goals for strategy and bad strategic objectives.

Prof Rumelt's explanations of where companies are going wrong are bracing and his prescriptions for good strategy – for example: diagnose critical challenges, set a guiding policy to deal with them, then take coherent action to accomplish your goals – have a simple force. But I fear few executives will take his medicine.

One reason is that they fear the accusation of inconsistency. Incumbents, unwilling to be dubbed flip-floppers, tend to stick with their bad strategy. Shareholders, instead of allowing an established chief executive to change his or her mind, change the chief executive, heralding the inevitable strategic review and potentially doubling the disruption.

A second reason for strategic failure is that leaders grow obsessed with dealmaking. Companies are brought to the public markets too soon and, once listed, pursue growth by acquisition – an option that should always be considered guilty until proved innocent, according to Prof Rumelt. My remedial starting point would be to outlaw the term 'strategic review' when the exercise is conducted by a friendly investment bank with an interest in recommending a fee-generating deal at the end of the process.

Last, executives succumb to leadership by 'vision'. This is the kind of missionary zeal – 'our strategic goal is to win' – that Lou Gerstner seemed to have consigned to the strategy-shredder in 1993, when he told reporters that 'the last thing IBM needs right now is a vision'.

In *Good Strategy/Bad Strategy*, Prof Rumelt dismisses 'ritual recitations [that] tap into a deep human capacity to believe that intensely focused desire is magically rewarded'. In person, he sounds more depressed about the trend. He recently asked his students to write down why companies were successful. Eight out of 10 offered a version of the answer that it was because those companies' leaders had vision. 'Where is this coming from?' he grumbles. Certainly not from the clear strategic thinking that won victory for Hannibal at Cannae two millennia ago.[10]

Source: Hill, A. (2011) Strategies founder on fluff and buzzwords, *Financial Times*, 13 June 2011.
© The Financial Times Limited 2011. All Rights Reserved.

Some readers took issue after that column with Prof Rumelt's Cannae example. Was this not a case of tactics rather than strategy? I wondered for a while whether better insights into how strategy and tactics intersect might be found in the military itself. What I found surprising, though, when I looked into how battlefield practice had evolved over the past century and a half, was how far ahead of business military leaders were when it came to developing the sorts of flexible approaches now needed at many civilian organisations and companies.

Business lessons from the front line

By Andrew Hill

Financial Times October 8, 2012

Jeff Bezos is on a mission to seek out and destroy military metaphors at work. 'You target your customers,' Amazon's chief executive told an audience in New York last year. 'I'm, like, what? Why would you do that? That doesn't make any sense.'

Such jargon – attacks on markets, broadsides against competition, war chests for acquisitions – reflects business's deep attachment to military parallels. In part, this is fantasy. Which male executive has not occasionally imagined he is a field commander planning an assault across enemy territory, rather than a middle manager performing a discounted cash flow calculation on a factory project, or preparing to pitch a dog food commercial? In part, however, it is good business.

Many companies like to hire military veterans (including Amazon, which boasts of being named the number one 'military-friendly' employer), a growing number of consultancies and management trainers sell themselves as providers of expertise learnt on the literal frontline, and strategists from Sun Tzu to Carl von Clausewitz can still add an exciting whiff of cordite to sterile presentations.

To the civilian outsider, this looks like a paradox. Command-and-control leadership is increasingly old-fashioned. Management innovators advocate loosening or even inverting corporate structures. Modern managers seem to have less to learn from traditional parade-ground virtues of discipline, uniformity and hierarchy, and more from subversive barracks backchat.

But important elements of this management revolution have already come to the armed forces, which helps explain why many companies are investing in army surplus techniques and personnel.

When I mentioned the old command-and-control military stereotype to the urbane former British army general Sir Michael Rose, he gently reminded me that, since at least the 1980s, European armed forces had adopted a 'mission command' approach – which lays out for officers in the field the why and the what of their mission, but leaves the how to them. The roots of the technique go even further back, to *Auftragstaktik*, developed in the 19th century by the Prussian army, an institution hardly known for its flexible, let-it-all-hang-out attitude.

The important lessons for business are very similar to those taught by management revolutionaries. Much of the time, leaders must trust juniors to take decisions without first reporting back up the chain to headquarters.

Celia Swanson, senior vice-president of talent development for Walmart in the US, says the 'aha moment' for her came when she recognised the 21st-century military approach was 'not about command and control [but] about how to develop others to be able to sustain the culture and community once the military leave'. When the retailer – another big recruiter of veterans – wanted to accelerate development of managers to match the growth of its store network, it built a 'leadership academy'. It is modelled on a military staff training college, following advice from Royal Marine commando-turned-consultant Damian McKinney.

His group, McKinney Rogers, and Skarbek, a new advisory outfit advised by Gen Rose, stress the mission command approach. It fits well into the 'execution' school of management. But that doesn't mean business can learn nothing from military strategy. Officers and business leaders who have contributed to *In Business and Battle*, a new book on the parallels, point out that modern military alliances have to be, if anything, more complex, more collaborative and more adaptable than many business combinations. 'In the old days, in war, [the mission] was black-and-white,' Gen Rose points out. 'Now, in peacekeeping and nation-building, it's a grey area.'

Old notions of military discipline and order are still a powerful selling point. Mr McKinney has just published *The Commando Way*, a manual for business execution, and his consultancy's branding makes it look more like an international peacekeeping force. It is also clearly absurd to suggest the world's armies, navies and air forces are now run like hippy collectives. But ex-military executives have a point when they say the tradition-steeped military institutions that trained them are less hidebound by hierarchy than many of the companies that now hire them.[11]

Source: Hill, A. (2012) Business lessons from the front line, *Financial Times*, 8 October 2012.
© The Financial Times Limited 2012. All Rights Reserved.

One of the paradoxes of strategy these days, is that it must be conducted at speed (as Amec's Samir Brikho, mentioned in the introduction to this chapter, acknowledged). The fortresses of competitive advantage can no longer be defended for long, if at all, as author and business school professor Rita Gunther McGrath explained to me in 2013.

Perpetual pilots are the new goal for strategy

By Andrew Hill

Financial Times July 1, 2013

Industries are in flux. Google's driverless cars are waiting at the intersection of internal combustion and search engines. Payment companies such as M-Pesa, Stripe and PayPal are testing the locks on banks' safe deposit boxes. Samsung, Apple and Google's Android have put Black-Berry and Nokia on hold. If you are the chief executive of a carmaker, financial institution or mobile phone maker and you are not yet worrying about the blurred edges of what was once a clearly demarcated border between sectors, you are lost.

Yet corporate cavemen still trigger the smugness alarm with statements such as 'I don't want any surprises' or 'don't bring me a problem unless you've got a solution'.

Rita Gunther McGrath, of Columbia Business School, says such comments are characteristic of leaders who think they have found a 'competitive advantage' – the holy grail of strategists since Michael Porter defined it in 1985, in his book of the same name.

You question the solidity of Prof Porter's work at your peril. When I asked him in 2011[12] whether the greatest economic and financial crisis in 75 years had shaken his theories, he was adamant they were 'more and more and more fundamentally important and visible'. But Prof McGrath's new book – provocatively entitled *The End of Competitive Advantage* – is a battering ram aimed straight at the door of Prof Porter's Harvard-based Institute for Strategy and Competitiveness.

As she told me last week, chief executives who cling to the illusion of competitive advantage are 'resisting the reality' of 21st-century corporate existence: fluctuating competition (and competitors), short-lived opportunities, constant challenge.

The danger with tearing down the Porter pillars is that companies will be left sitting in the rubble, without landmarks to help them find a new path. But Prof McGrath offers a guide through the volatility that includes a policy of constant, systematic early-stage innovation.

Peter Sands, Standard Chartered's chief executive, summed up the approach well in the FT yesterday,[13] when he outlined the threat to risk-averse, regulation-bound banks from nimbler competitors and a solution that involves 'generating more ideas, implementing them more swiftly, [and] being quicker to discard the ones that do not work'.

told me companies needed 'ambidextrous' executives – good at forward thinking and advance planning but also capable of acting on his mantra that 'execution is strategic'. He politely dodged the question of what he would say if a certified strategist presented his diploma in a job interview. But I suspect when Steve Ballmer hired Mr Turner in 2005 – in the middle of the strategic and operational mess that was Windows Vista – it was his record as a successful executive at Walmart that swung the job his way, rather than his BSc in Management.

That said, some of the reasons underpinning the SPS initiative look good. In the fat years, many companies lost sight of their strategies, or even their business models. They tailored both to short-term goals and used financial and accounting tools to achieve them, becoming obsessed with their relative profitability rather than their long-term cash flow. Failure to think strategically and inability to disentangle strategy from mere 'vision' left many ill-prepared for the inevitable crisis. At the same time, as Gary Hamel – surely a shoo-in for a future honorary fellowship in strategy – pointed out to me, many universities have allowed their own management research to drift off into financial exotica or business esoterica. The former are potentially dangerous, the latter practically irrelevant to employers of new-minted MBAs. Sharpened up, the new profession could offer clearer guidelines about how to set and measure a successful strategy.

Still, I remain doubtful. In 2008, as Lehman Brothers was imploding, Harvard's Nitin Nohria (now dean of the business school) and Rakesh Khurana argued that management should become 'a true profession',[17] complete with a Hippocratic oath. Certified managers who had 'mastered a body of knowledge and [were] current in their knowledge of new ideas in business' would command a premium, they wrote.

One strong objection to their idea was that the role of manager, unlike that of a doctor or a lawyer, is general, hard to define and of variable focus – one day analysing sales, the next straightening out a supply chain, the third plotting acquisitions. Strategy is a narrower discipline, but the SPS says it 'necessarily cuts across all business functions' and, as a result, should be an 'open' profession. But while the alternative of closed shops and feuding trade associations is undesirable, this openness makes strategy sound worryingly like, well, journalism – a 'profession' where almost anyone gets called *Dottore*.

The jargon-clogged world of strategy needs some order – greater consensus about its most useful tools, a regularly updated body of knowledge, perhaps some standards of best practice. These are worthy goals. But a new class of certified strategists? No, *grazie*.[18]

FT   *Source:* Hill, A. (2012) Experience trumps exams for strategists, *Financial Times*, 12 March 2012.
© The Financial Times Limited 2012. All Rights Reserved.

Strategy – as the Shell scenarios suggest – is inevitably entwined with an assessment of future risks. But the dangers involved in getting those risk assessments wrong were underlined in Britain in 2014. Businesses that expected Scotland would vote strongly against independence from the rest of the UK were taken by surprise when polls in the run-up to the referendum showed the gap was narrower than forecast. The outcome was, in the end, a fairly comfortable victory for the No campaign (perhaps affected by the late intervention of some big companies, which pointed to the economic risks of a split).

Yet the near miss was a reminder to leaders that political risk is often closer to home than forecasters think. Another example was the 2014 British Budget, which coincided with those knife-edge referendum reforms and contained a shock announcement of pension reforms. It triggered this column.

When a haven harbours unseen risk

By Andrew Hill

Financial Times March 24, 2014

If you had asked board directors at the beginning of last week which of two situations – the stand-off between Russia and Ukraine in Crimea, and the forthcoming British Budget – was politically riskier, they would have chosen the first. But for a few insurers involved in the lucrative business of offering annuities to pensioners, Britain turned out to be the more perilous place after George Osborne, the UK chancellor, astounded them by announcing reforms that could cut the size of that market by 90 per cent.

The Crimean crisis, for all its unpredictability, fits into the category of political risk that risk analysts love to analyse, risk managers to manage and insurers to insure against. If a capricious commander-in-chief orders men in fatigues in faraway places to do something that disrupts your supply chain or shuts down your factory, you may not like it, but the chances are you have braced yourselves for it. But if a minister in an industrialised country marches in and annexes your company's profit forecasts overnight, it may come as a shock. It should not. 'Safe' countries are riskier than they look.

Much recent economic growth has been concentrated in places where political and regulatory risk is high. Control Risks estimated the share of global output generated in riskier countries, coloured amber or red on its 2014 political RiskMap,[19] had more than doubled to 35 per cent in the preceding decade. Multinationals have of necessity focused their investment and attention there. As a result, Richard Fenning, the consultancy's chief executive, reckons boards now 'fixate on political risk as what can be covered by a Lloyd's of London insurance policy'.

Such an approach is understandable if you are Twitter, facing a ban in Turkey, Repsol, the Spanish company whose majority stake in Argentina's YPF was nationalised in 2012, or Glencore, which has mining operations in volatile areas overseen by trigger-happy local authorities. Before listing in 2011, Glencore outlined potential geopolitical threats that included 'terrorism, civil war, guerrilla activities, military repression, civil disorder, crime, workforce instability, change in government policy or the ruling party, economic or other sanctions imposed by other countries, extreme fluctuations in currency exchange rates or high inflation'.

'Risk factors' in companies' share-listing documents are a bit like 'may contain nuts' labels on food products – worthless to allergy-prone investors until their shares go into anaphylactic shock, at which point the company can say: 'You can't say we didn't warn you'. But even so, it is significant that the political risk sections in the 2013 prospectuses of Partnership Assurance and Just Retirement – the two British annuity companies worst hit by last week's Budget shockwave – consisted of virtually identical cut-and-paste legalese. The assumption was that the main threats to their business would be regulatory and incremental, not legislative and far-reaching.[20]

G7 countries undoubtedly look like more stable places to do business than, say, Argentina, Turkey or Russia. But ask the directors of BP, HSBC and Standard Chartered – all of which have been flagellated by the American public and politicians following recent operational disasters – whether they assessed correctly the political risk of investing in and trading with the US.

Similarly, most executives would have listed Scottish independence or British withdrawal from the EU as outside chances until a few years ago. Now, even General Electric – a multinational that knows a lot about political risk – is giving warning about the potentially unpleasant consequences of Scotland breaking away or Britain quitting the EU. With a UK general election next spring, boards should

➡

be modelling the risks of potentially sweeping changes in energy and immigration policy, too.

Last week's unexpected pension reform 'probably has got a number of risk officers readjusting how they think about political risk', one affected insurer's head of risk ruefully admitted to me. But political risk equations should always multiply the scale of investment by the likelihood of a government springing a surprise. One salutary and important lesson is that even in supposedly safer countries – which, after all, still account for two-thirds of output – not every political risk is manageable, insurable or even predictable.[21]

Source: Hill, A. (2014) When a haven harbours unseen risk, *Financial Times*, 24 March 2014.
© The Financial Times Limited 2014. All Rights Reserved.

As Shell's long history of scenario planning suggests, this is not a new problem. Companies have always needed some capacity to react quickly and retain flexibility, even as the circumstances are changing. In 1982, for instance, the then president of Exxon, speaking as the price of oil declined from its post oil-shock high, said: 'Trying to forecast oil demand, supply and price in today's market is like trying to paint the wings of an aeroplane in flight. Even if one succeeds in covering the subject, it's unlikely to be a tidy job.'

Accelerating technology change has, however, increased the number of course corrections required during the tenure of any executive, even if the overall strategic destination remains the same. As Herminia Ibarra has written in her book *Act Like a Leader, Think Like a Leader*, even planning a transition to becoming a leader requires executives to be adaptable. Too often, she says, leaders are told to start at A and proceed in a straight line to B, the objective they have set themselves. But 'B changes as we approach it'. Here, on a similar theme, is a column I wrote welcoming in a nervous New Year in 2012.

Three cheers for new year trepidation

By Andrew Hill

Financial Times January 2, 2012

Hurrah for uncertainty! Three cheers for trepidation! As the world tiptoes gingerly into 2012, let's celebrate the fallibility of forecasting and the perils of prediction.

Why? First, because uncertainty will not dissipate soon, so businesses might as well try to make the best of what little they do know. Second, because an excess of certainty got us into this predicament. A little new year caution may be welcome.

Some of the steps taken by managers to offset dangers ahead are worryingly circular, however. I was surprised, for example, at the number of top executives and directors who, in a recent survey for Lloyd's , the London insurance market, said the most effective risk management action they had taken over the past three years was . . . to put in place a risk management team.

Other countermeasures can prove counterproductive. In June 2010, McKinsey consultant Lowell Bryan suggested companies should prepare for the 'high probability of future financial shocks' by erring on the side of 'being overcapitalised, overliquid, and overprepared',[22] while also engaging in 'serious scenario planning' about 'unthinkable' events. Sensible. But the effort of holding this brace position for the past 18 months, while some of those unthinkable events unfolded, would have induced paralysis in most business leaders by now.

As Leif Johansson, chairman of Ericsson and current head of the European Round Table of Industrialists, told the *Financial Times* last month, on the eve of the European summit: 'Uncertainty has that effect: on many, many individual accounts, customers are saying "Let's wait a little". And the trouble with that wait-and-see attitude . . . is that it takes us into a recession, quicker and steeper than we would have expected.'

He knows from grim experience what he's talking about. In his old job, as chief executive of Volvo, he witnessed the extraordinary period in late 2008 when more customers in Europe were cancelling orders for its trucks than placing them.

Even some of Mr Bryan's sensible measures could inadvertently add to future uncertainty. Absolute Strategy Research, an independent group of macro analysts, points out that in the US and Europe, the corporate savings rate has increased to levels not seen for decades, as public sector deficits have ballooned. The hoarding could reflect justifiable caution but if it persists, ASR suggests, governments may start accusing large companies of 'rent-seeking' behaviour and may even penalise those that are seen to have accumulated 'excessive' cash.

As for scenario planning, it has its uses, but, as another chief executive of a large European industrial company told me recently in relation to the fate of the euro: 'We have plan Bs [for potential break-up of the currency], but there are only so many plan Bs you can make.'

As executives' reluctance to commit themselves grows, so the appetite of outsiders to know about their future plans increases. Investors are now far more interested in the 'outlook' section of the company report than in the backward-looking summary of the historic results. But in their public statements, most chief executives hide behind a 'lack of visibility', adding to the general nervousness.

Let them instead embrace uncertainty and accept that it is unrealistic to expect all clouds to lift and the way ahead to become clear. Business leaders need to count on their ability to be the one-eyed man in the land of the blind – a proverb recast by Richard Rumelt in his book *Good Strategy/Bad Strategy*: 'If you can peer into the fog of change and see 10 per cent more clearly than others see, then you may gain an edge.'

Merely peering is not enough, though, if you do not move forward. So, in the spirit of circularity, let me offer the mini-roundabout, that peculiarly British innovation in traffic management, as my metaphor for sensible strategy in times of peril. The mini-roundabout instils just enough uncertainty in drivers to encourage them to reduce speed at junctions, but not so much doubt as to cause gridlock. When it comes to assessing future risks, it may not have the romantic appeal of certain rare waterfowl popularised by Nassim Nicholas Taleb but, as a reminder neither to accelerate blindly into the unknown, nor to stall for fear of collisions, it could prove more useful.[23]

 Source: Hill, A. (2012) Three cheers for new year trepidation, *Financial Times*, 2 January 2012.
© The Financial Times Limited 2012. All Rights Reserved.

Leadership lessons:

1. Understand the link between strategy and execution.

2. Avoid setting plans in stone – they will undoubtedly be overwhelmed by events.

3. Ensure that you are looking at the horizon, not just the immediate future . . .

4. . . . but do not allow horizon-scanning to become a substitute for decision-making.

5. Remember that risk – particularly political risk – may be closer to home than you suspect.

6. Remain open to the possibility of course correction.

7. Remember that nobody can see the future with perfect clarity. If they do, it is probably a fluke.

Moving

A leader without followers is a contradiction in terms. But many executives given charge of a team, division or company assume that authority comes with the title and that followers will fall in behind them as a result. The reality is quite different. The ability to motivate a team – to move it – is a critical leadership skill.

Unfortunately, too often, leaders pick up the traditional tools of management to motivate their team members: bonuses, the promise of promotion, the threat of dismissal. 'Softer' approaches can be at least as effective: laying out a clear sense of purpose, giving positive feedback, even the offer of a simple thank-you. But since regulators and policymakers have made bonuses the focus of their investigation of the causes and consequences of the 2008–09 financial crisis, let me start there.

Bosses are blinded by their bonus obsession

By Andrew Hill

Financial Times February 7, 2011

'The interests of the corporation and its stockholders are best served by making key employees partners in the corporation's prosperity . . . Each individual should be rewarded in proportion to his contribution to the profit of his own division and of the corporation as a whole.'

(Alfred P. Sloan, *My Years With General Motors*)

Simple. Yet in spite of the logic of Sloan's prescription and nearly a century of experience since the GM bonus plan was adopted in 1918, companies are no closer to getting executive pay right. In fact, with each tweak of a pay package or recalibration of the 'rules', they edge further from the goal.

Such is the paucity of original ideas – in inverse proportion to the surfeit of people paid to think them up – that the best some experts can offer is that to reach a perfect alignment of pay, performance and corporate and community interest, you wouldn't start from here.

➡

The problem with bonuses is that corporate paymasters think they are more important to staff than the staff themselves do. Recent research by PwC, the professional services firm, and the London School of Economics suggests the value that executives attach to incentives dwindles the longer payments are deferred, the more ambiguous or complex the plan, and the less control they have over how to meet targets. If employees think rewards are allocated arbitrarily or unfairly, bonuses undermine their motivation.

In finance – where bonuses are valued to an obsessive degree – the risk that they will distort behaviour is even greater. 'If you frame [your environment] in terms of money, you think only money matters,' says David De Cremer, professor of behavioural business ethics at Rotterdam School of Management. Instead of focusing on doing the job well, bankers focus on the reward for doing it. At best, bank employees jump through hoops to impress their bosses in bonus season. At worst, they behave unethically to polish performance and hit targets.

But where the worst financial crisis since the 1930s has failed to change this culture, it is hard to imagine mere pay reform will succeed. Amending the rules may make things worse. That was the case in the 1990s, after the US Congress capped at $1m the part of an executive's salary on which a company could claim tax deductions, prompting an explosion of stock option use – and abuse. It will be the case again with new rules to defer bank bonuses and claw back rewards for deals that later go bad.

Unfortunately, the alternatives sound utopian. The intrinsic motivation of many bankers is the cut and thrust of the deal or the excitement of the big trade. Prof De Cremer hopes they can be made to seek motivation in the underlying value of their profession and their duty to society. A worthy goal – but one that will take generations to achieve, if it is possible at all.

Instead, managers should set aside their blueprints and their Black-Scholes option calculators and return to first principles.

The quest for the ideal incentive package is, as behavioural scientists' increasing interest suggests, a human problem more than a mathematical one. Finding an answer takes time.

David Cote, chief executive of Honeywell, the US industrial group, with 122,000 global employees, reviews the performance of his top 200 people at least three times a year.

Tailoring incentives in the right way also requires flexibility. Mr Cote's basic notion that pay is about 'fairness, not formula' is as good a starting point as any. Of course, where money is involved, one person's fair outcome is another's travesty, as the gulf between Barclays and the rest of the world's view of Bob Diamond's pay package shows. That means progress will be made only by trial and error. If poorly supervised or insufficiently transparent, bonuses will be open to abuse. Even Sloan had to ask GM directors to adjust its incentive plan after the Depression gutted bonuses, a move that would put modern governance police on high alert.

But these are not reasons to ditch incentive pay altogether, as long as managers recognise its limitations. Bonuses play their part in motivating staff on specific tasks or in certain areas, such as sales. But most employees are driven by a mix of goodwill, inner motivation and survival instinct.

If employers stopped obsessing about bonuses as a silver bullet to improve performance, they might be amazed to discover how much could be achieved by encouraging staff with a fair salary, regular feedback and just treatment.[24]

Source: Hill, A. (2011) Bosses are blinded by their bonus obsession, *Financial Times*, 7 February 2011.
© The Financial Times Limited 2011. All Rights Reserved.

With the rest of the world obsessed about recalibrating bonuses, a cadre of researchers – backed by innovative corporate leaders – has done creative work on the effectiveness of other types of motivation. I met one such academic – Teresa Amabile of Harvard – on a visit to the university's business school in September 2011.

Tiny bursts of joy pave the way to BHAGs

By Andrew Hill

Financial Times September 12, 2011

Consider how many BHAGs you have achieved over your career. 'Big hairy audacious goal' is the memorable (if faintly bizarre) phrase coined by Jim Collins and Jerry Porras 15 years ago[25] for a visionary strategic objective that can inspire a whole team.

It is in the nature of such shaggy milestones that companies will reach them only rarely. BHAGs have a 10-to-30-year lead-time, according to the authors. When executives who clock up as few as seven years at the same company are described as 'veterans', the chance that many staff will be present from vision through to realisation must be low.

No wonder that, in their effort to motivate individual team-members, companies still fall back on more workaday tools: pay-rises and bonuses to encourage good work; deadlines to keep that work on schedule; perks to make the journey agreeable, or merely bearable.

These sources of 'extrinsic' motivation are an unavoidable part of most corporate cultures. But they can also destroy workers' fragile love of the job – the intrinsic motivation that underpins creativity and success – or drive staff in the wrong strategic or, worse, ethical direction.

If companies hit big goals infrequently, and the incentives for reaching them have toxic side-effects, it would be better for them to find other ways to encourage worker engagement. Teresa Amabile of Harvard Business School and her husband Steven Kramer, a developmental psychologist, believe an obvious, but often overlooked, approach is for managers to remove barriers to day-to-day progress.

Their insight is supported by research based on 12,000 daily diary entries by workers at seven companies, which became an article and now a book, *The Progress Principle*. These intimate accounts of what teams were thinking showed that even quite small steps forward at work generated a burst of joy (yes, it sounds hokey – but they maintain it's the correct word) that inspired creative work over a period of days.

The diaries show, in one case, that a team-member demoralised by rounds of redundancies among her workmates was quickly re-energised by the success of an urgent project, even though she had to cancel her holiday. It didn't take much for senior managers to sustain this virtuous cycle – an on-site appearance, a bottle of branded mineral water for the hard-working staff and some words of encouragement.

Appealing though the idea is, it sparked my scepticism. Last week, Bob Dudley, BP's chief executive, sent an e-mail to staff urging them to look away from negative headlines and focus on the fact that the oil company was 'making real, solid and measurable progress to build the new foundation for a strong and successful future'. Aren't bosses guilty of whistling in the dark if they extol progress when the company has suffered profound strategic setbacks?

Prof Amabile told me it was essential for managers not to over-emphasise achievements, let alone fabricate them. Employees would see straight through such a ploy. 'You can't do this if there's no progress: that would look fake,' she said. In that regard, the extent to which Mr Dudley's memo galvanises staff will depend just how 'real, solid and measurable' its advances are.

Even then, if the strategic direction of a company is wrong, no amount of day-to-day progress will rescue it. Similarly, if staff don't find their work meaningful, they won't value even quite large achievements.

'Small wins' lack the hirsute macho appeal of the Collins-Porras goals. But the theory feels right. As the workplace chronicles attest, the positive impact of incremental advances endures. What is more, most of the catalysts for employees' intrinsic motivation – basic resources (not gimmicky perks), autonomy, adequate time for the project in hand – are cheap or even free.

As for the challenging economic backdrop, I met Prof Amabile in Harvard on the day that Barack Obama was due to sell his $450bn job-creation plan to Congress. Most of the embattled US president's inauguration day BHAGs look further off than ever. A few daily advances in the American workplace won't bring them much closer. But the cumulative effect of instilling a progress principle could, over time, be large.

Meanwhile, if there is one person in the US who needs some small wins – and the consequent boost in morale and creative thinking – it is the president himself.[26]

Source: Hill, A. (2011) Tiny bursts of joy pave the way to BHAGs, *Financial Times*, 12 September 2011.
© The Financial Times Limited 2011. All Rights Reserved.

A point that always strikes me when I visit Silicon Valley is the degree to which entrepreneurs there are motivated by a desire to do something revolutionary. I recall meeting one start-up founder who was quite prepared to junk his company if it turned out merely to achieve incremental improvements in the way we lived or worked (as it happens, he 'pivoted' – changing the business model of his company – and managed to sell the whole venture for millions to a bigger company with a less lofty goal).

What, though, would someone who had achieved such a world-changing breakthrough make of Prof Amabile's insights into the motivational power of smaller, closer-range targets and achievements?

We should stop trying to change the world

By Andrew Hill

Financial Times March 26, 2012

Given the essentially mundane nature of most jobs, few workers will ever live up to mission statements that urge them to 'change the world'.

Vint Cerf is one of the few people who indisputably has changed it. Nearly 40 years ago, he co-designed the ubiquitous TCP/IP software protocols that allow closed computer networks to communicate with each other and form a 'network of networks': the internet.

For a self-confessed Star Trek enthusiast who is working on an interplanetary internet project with Nasa and has the title of Google's 'chief internet evangelist', Mr Cerf is reassuringly down to earth. Launching an Economist technology conference last week in London, he described what he started in the 1970s as 'an experiment' that continues to this day.

Would he have been more successful, or more motivated, had his bosses at the US Department of Defense's Advanced Research Projects Agency (Darpa) told him to change the world? I don't think so. More important, he doesn't, either.

The distance between the task in hand and an overly ambitious future goal is often so great that the path is certain to be a tortuous one – and the outcome possibly different from that envisaged.

For instance, some forecasts of how networks would change business 'turned out to be oddly wrong', Mr Cerf told me. When Darpa engineers invented electronic mail in 1971, they expected travel budgets to decrease because employees would not need to meet as often in person. Five years later, travel spending had increased fourfold. Thanks to email, users were working with more people, from further afield, on bigger projects. Face-to-face meetings were still needed, and they were more expensive to organise.

As web connections continue to proliferate and speed up, the capacity for business to tackle ever larger challenges and form larger teams to meet them is increasing. So is the need to understand how to energise and direct them. Google now has 30,000 employees, compared with 5,000 when Mr Cerf joined in 2005. Larry Page, its founder who again took up the chief executive role last year, has narrowed the number of products and services on which the search group is working. Yet tasks are still divided into projects that can be handled by groups of no more than five to 10 people. (Similarly, at Amazon, Jeff Bezos limits teams to those small enough to be fed with two pizzas.) This focus improves accountability and clarity – in a small group, no one can avoid pulling their weight and no one can claim they don't know what the goal is.

No grandiose mission statement is needed to motivate such teams. I've written before how even quite small advances towards a goal energise staff, provided they are granted autonomy and the work itself is rewarding. Meaningful work doesn't have to be about outlining the meaning of life. Mr Cerf says he believes 'the best way for the "next big thing" to happen is [for teams] to be challenged to solve a previously unsolvable problem'.

He cites Google's attempt to devise a self-driving car. But the engineers who were told to put a man on the moon, the technicians who rose to Ratan Tata's challenge to produce a 'one-lakh' car for India, or the scientists hunting for subatomic particles at the Cern Large Hadron Collider were also pointed towards a practical, clearly stated goal.

Mr Cerf was followed on to the podium at last week's conference by another veteran engineer and inventor, Bran Ferren, who urged the audience to have 'a passionate vision about what you think will change people's lives'.

But Mr Cerf responded, quietly, that in laying the foundations of the internet, he and his colleagues 'weren't driven by a belief we were going to change the world; we were driven by a desire to solve a particular problem'.

Many bosses hope to inspire their workforce to aim high. Mr Page is one of them. There's nothing wrong with that. As Mr Ferren warned, 'it's possible to aim low and miss'. But to work doggedly towards a single, defined objective is noble, whether or not the task is larded with extravagant claims about its potential impact. I favour more missions but fewer statements. And who knows, 40 years on, today's humble problem-solvers might find themselves lauded as the founding fathers of the next big thing.[27]

Source: Hill, A. (2012) We should stop trying to change the world, *Financial Times*, 26 March 2012.
© The Financial Times Limited 2012. All Rights Reserved.

If one part of motivating people is finding the right carrot, another must be using the correct stick. 'Forced ranking' – the discipline that companies should always aim to ditch their worst performers – has fascinated me since I followed the latter stages of Jack Welch's career at General Electric in 1999 and 2000.

Mr Welch was an advocate of the idea and so was Enron, which called it 'ranking and yanking', until it was itself destroyed by fraud. The unintended consequences of such a system are, however, gravely demotivating.

Forced ranking is a relic of an HR tool

By Andrew Hill

Financial Times July 16, 2012

Around the turn of the last century, I heard Jack Welch recount how he had visited a clothing store on New York's Fifth Avenue to buy a sweater. A sales manager approached the then boss of General Electric, said he was a fan, and in an embarrassed whisper, sought his advice. Was it essential to get rid of the worst-performing 10 per cent of his staff every year, even though his own team consisted of just three people? 'Of course,' Mr Welch replied breezily.

Bracing certainty was – and still is – the former GE chief's stock in trade. I also once saw him frighten a group of business students by pointing out that they could surely all identify their worst-performing classmates. In business, he believed, it was just 'false kindness' to keep laggards on into their 50s, only then to sack them all.

Mr Welch calls the bell curve used to illustrate his system a 'vitality curve', making it sound like an energy diet. I had assumed that over the past decade, companies had tested his old certainties, found them wanting and driven a stake through the heart of such forced ranking.

I was wrong. For the latest edition of Vanity Fair magazine, Kurt Eichenwald analysed Microsoft's 'lost decade'[28] and pinned some of the blame for the technology group's loss of momentum on a similar-sounding system of 'stack ranking'. He says the company divided teams according to a 20-70-10 ratio for six-monthly performance reviews and used that curve to determine 'promotions, bonuses, or just survival'. 'Every current and former Microsoft employee I interviewed – every one – cited stack ranking as the most destructive process inside of Microsoft,' writes Mr Eichenwald.

I've written here why I think career reviews are important. I won't recant. Most companies differentiate between staff and expect a distribution of performance. But if appraisals have a bad name, it is partly due to the crude way such assessments are enforced. Unite, the British trade union, is convinced not only that the vitality curve survives, but that it may now be more popular among UK managers than with their US counterparts.

Elsewhere, the system may have mellowed, as the returns from forced ranking diminish. GE no longer ranks people the Jack Welch way. Microsoft (which would not comment on the Vanity Fair article) has in recent years simplified and amended its system based on employee feedback. At consultancies, where highly ambitious, self-confident, strongly motivated, thick-skinned employees compete for primacy, 'rank and yank' continues to thrive, though it has the more user-friendly title of 'up or out'.

But the few benefits cited by fans – it creates all-star teams and continually raises the bar for performance – are far outweighed by the disadvantages, which are:

■ Horse-trading. Apart from the lobbying and politicking before any review, the threat of grading on the curve encourages managers to waste time trading favours with each other. The Vanity Fair article describes drawn-out meetings at which Microsoft team leaders would haggle over names, using whiteboard grids and Post-it notes, until they had met their overall divisional targets.

■ Infighting. Far from increasing the desire of staff to work in high-performing teams, the vitality curve sucks the life out of collaboration. Why choose to work with the company's stars if they push you down into the bottom 10 per cent?

■ 'Big fish' syndrome. No matter how large the group to which the curve is applied, companies end up comparing like with unlike, punishing those whose talents may simply be ill-matched to their current role, and rewarding staff who, in a better-performing team, would look less impressive.

■ Bad hiring. Managers no longer have the incentive to make their recruitment decisions work because they know they can move low performers on once a year.

■ Short-termism. 'People planned their days and their years around the review, rather than around products,' one software designer told Mr Eichenwald. Most teams improve as they learn how to work together. Lack of continuity, or even the threat of it, impedes such advances.

Add the fact that it is costly (all those forced exits) and puts companies at risk of litigation (Ford, Goodyear and Sprint have all faced age discrimination suits linked to forced ranking), and the system looks like a relic. Sorry, Jack. Where the ghost of the vitality curve lives on, exorcism is long overdue.[29]

Source: Hill, A. (2012) Forced ranking is a relic of an HR tool, *Financial Times*, 16 July 2012.
© The Financial Times Limited 2012. All Rights Reserved.

Microsoft eliminated its 'stack ranking' system in November 2013 and said it would introduce a new system aimed at improving teamwork and collaboration. But the practice lives on – notably at Amazon, which, according to a recent investigation by the New York Times – disputed by its founder Jeff Bezos – combines forced ranking with aggressive use of data and technology tools to encourage team members to feed good, and bad, comments about their colleagues' work ethic to their superiors.[30] I would encourage leaders to follow a different trend: towards more subtle motivational tools, some of which may be as simple as saying 'Thanks'.

Thank you can be the hardest words

By Andrew Hill

Financial Times November 26, 2012

A charity fundraiser told me recently that it was a rule of thumb in philanthropic circles that you should thank donors seven times.

Apart from online references to 'tradition', 'common wisdom' and, inevitably, 'Chinese custom', I've found no empirical research to support this magic number. Some experts on charitable giving have never heard of the idea; those who have are divided about whether it is even a useful maxim.

There is, however, plenty of research – much of which is revisited in the US at this time of year to add scientific rigour to Thanksgiving – into whether gratitude improves behaviour. The short answer: it does, a lot. That makes it all the more perplexing that, in most workplaces, simple (and cheap) thank-yous are undervalued as motivational tools, while complex cash-based incentive packages abound.

This is not to imply that bosses never say thanks. But they mix messages and often offer public displays of gratitude when it's too late – the valued employee is leaving.

Steven Sinofsky, Microsoft's former Windows expert, is by most accounts an abrasive character; Steve Ballmer, the software group's head, is as hard-nosed as any chief executive. When the former quit unexpectedly this month, the latter wasted just 16 words saying how grateful he was for Mr Sinofsky's 'many years of work' before getting back to promoting Windows products.

Rakesh Kapoor of Reckitt Benckiser dispatched his chief financial officer, Liz Doherty, in September, with a brief thank-you – before pointing out how their working styles were not well matched. (Perhaps the clue was in his use of the phrase 'I want to thank Liz . . .' – a construction that always suggests to me the unspoken addition ' . . . but I just can't bring myself to do so'.)

For all I know, the unseen interaction between these corporate heavyweights before they parted ways was full of elaborate exchanges of gratitude. If it was, the research suggests it would have supercharged their contributions. In a version of the prisoner's dilemma game, psychologist David DeSteno and others found gratitude enhanced co-operative behaviour[31] – not only between the thanker and the thanked, but between the recipient and third parties.

Fellow academics Adam Grant and Francesca Gino suggest mere expressions of thanks make recipients feel valued[32] and could be 'sufficiently potent' to persuade them to redouble their efforts.

It is easy to come up with different ways of thanking work colleagues: from the boss's simple declaration of 'good job' in the lift up to the office, to her emailed and handwritten notes of congratulation, up to mentions in the annual report or the chairman's speech. Why, then, do leaders not use such low-cost tools more often, and why do followers regard them with suspicion?

It must be in part because purveyors of the workplace thank-you so often pollute its positive impact with less palatable messages, inviting cynicism.

For guidance, a thank-you is not:

■ A way of improving skills. Thanking an incompetent staff member for work only just up to standard may persuade him to work harder, but not better. That's what training is for.

■ An alternative to money or promotion. Cash is certainly a poor substitute for gratitude, but the reverse is also true. Profuse thanks may work once in lieu of a bonus. By the third or fourth year, the motivational effect of the thank-you letter tends to wear off.

■ An apology. 'Thank you for offering to cover for Joan (after I forgot she had asked for time off)': wrong. 'I'm sorry for leaving you in the lurch on Joan's day off – but thanks for covering': right.

■ An order, as in the hollow pre-gratitude of memos that begin: 'Thanks in advance for coming in over the holiday period to complete the project.'

As other studies have shown, people tend to give far more weight to negative communications than to positive ones. That suggests employers need to dispense proportionately more gratitude to offset the harsher news they often have to transmit.

Even if these confused signals are straightened out, academics, fundraisers, executives and workers agree on one golden rule: thank-yous have to be sincere. Quality, in short, trumps quantity. Thanks so much for reading.[33]

Source: Hill, A. (2012) Thank you can be the hardest words, *Financial Times*, 26 November 2012.
© The Financial Times Limited 2012. All Rights Reserved.

As an aside, it is worth recalling what Simon Hayes, chief executive of Peel Hunt, a City of London broker and adviser, told me about how his staff reacted to news of their bonuses before the financial crisis: 'With very few exceptions, no one ever dared to say "thank you".'

In tandem with the growth of a collaborative leadership approach has come the rise of 'purpose' as a means of motivation and retention of staff. It spread like a rash at the World Economic Forum in Davos – an annual platform for chief executives to talk to each other, and to the world, about the good things happening at their companies and to get away (relatively) unchallenged about the bad. I have concerns, however, about the gulf between principle and practice.

'Purpose' is the preachy new CEO buzzword

By Andrew Hill

Financial Times January 27, 2014

When Ellen Kullman, chief executive of DuPont, asked a contract worker on the production line making Kevlar, the fibre used in bulletproof vests, what he was doing, she got an unexpected response: 'We're saving lives.'

The comment underlined her conviction that a sense of purpose was far more effective at hiring, motivating and keeping staff than any corporate brand, vision or mission statement.

She was not the only chief executive at the World Economic Forum last week to use the term 'purpose', as business slowly battles to restore public trust. In making any company more resilient, 'the most important thing is to focus on purpose,' said Brian Moynihan, who is wrestling Bank of America into post-crisis shape. 'You have to be a purpose-driven organisation,' added Mark Weinberger, head of EY, one of the Big Four professional services groups.

But even chief executives differ on precisely what purpose is. If it cannot be expressed easily, I doubt they will make it stick. Yet if it can be boiled down to a general single sentence, to fit the many mundane tasks a company and its staff have to perform, I wonder how it differs from the much-derided, meaningless mission statement (Acme Widget: Meeting the Unmet Needs of Customers Everywhere).

One difference is that whereas chief executives (particularly new chief executives) can change missions and visions on a whim, purpose is far harder to shape. That is an advantage – if you can harness your company to your younger employees' search for meaning at work, you will gain their loyalty – but also a pitfall. For one thing, as young employees grow up, their reasons for going to work will change. For another, as Asia experts at Davos reminded me, in some faster-growing markets such as China, the imperative for workers to make money easily trumps purpose. If the Kevlar worker had responded 'I'm earning a decent wage to feed my family', would it have meant he was any less motivated to do a good job?

Another reason that purpose is double-edged is that it gives off a whiff of the sacred. But a purpose that sanctifies work can also quickly become sanctimonious. Precisely because purpose is important to workers and customers, they will be quick to punish executives who appear to diverge from its path. When academics Sandra Cha and Amy Edmondson studied a maverick advertising agency[34] with a charismatic leader a few years ago, they were surprised to discover that the same employees who had joined the company for its idealistic set of values were highly critical of its boss because they believed he was not living up to them. One reason was that the staff were interpreting the group's purpose slightly differently – and more broadly – than the chief executive intended; the researchers called it 'value expansion'.

One lesson is that even if purpose is more powerful than the old motivational methods, CEOs need a good explanation to hand when corporate reality clashes with the high-sounding values to which their staff are committed.

Facing such challenges, some chief executives must be tempted to return to simple pursuit of profit, or to assume that merely making good products well is sufficient. But such an attitude will not narrow the trust gap between business and the public. Unreliable products and services will undermine confidence in companies but customers and staff want companies to live up to higher standards of behaviour, too.

Dov Seidman, a consultant and advocate of 'principled performance', points to Johnson & Johnson's 70-year-old 'credo' as a model. It states that the healthcare company's first responsibility is to the doctors, nurses, patients, mothers and fathers who use its products and concludes: 'When we operate according to these principles, the stockholders should earn a fair return.' He is suspicious of companies that use purpose for marketing or recruitment. 'I want to know who is doing it to make money, and who is doing it because it is who they are,' he says.

As Ms Kullman points out: 'We had a vision and a mission and nobody understood what they were.' But the appearance of purpose in Davosspeak is a warning to executives that it could suffer the same fate, hollowed of meaning by a combination of overuse, abuse, breach of corporate promise and general cynicism.[35]

Source: Hill, A. (2014) 'Purpose' is the preachy new CEO buzzword, *Financial Times*, 27 January 2014.
© The Financial Times Limited 2014. All Rights Reserved.

Purpose is at the heart of the use of 'stories' to move and inspire staff. Stories, properly told, can lubricate a dry speech and leaven a difficult message. They offset an overdependence on data. But they also carry a number of risks. Leaders could become so committed to their own story that they start to twist reality to fit the plot. One way to avoid this is to invite staff to contribute to the narrative; another is to lighten the tale with a little self-deprecation. Just before the same World Economic Forum where I met Ms Kullman, Dutch banker Gerrit Zalm made a surprising and original presentation to his staff.

Bosses in drag can set a good tone at the top

By Andrew Hill

Financial Times January 20, 2014

In the dreary annals of presentations about corporate values, ABN Amro chairman Gerrit Zalm's recent performance for the bank's annual cabaret as his brothel-keeping 'sister' Priscilla will take some beating.

Personally, I would like to see more bank bosses in drag. Not that I am particularly excited by the idea of Goldman Sachs's Lloyd Blankfein in Priscilla-style heels and red wig, or Barclays' Antony Jenkins in gold elbow-length gloves and a blue dress with matching Dame Edna Everage-style glasses. It is rather that Mr Zalm could give his peers a lesson in the use of humour as a vehicle for a serious corporate message.

What is more, a dose of what the Dutch call *zelfspot*, roughly translated as self-mockery, is just what leaders need on the eve of this week's festival of serious-seeming people taking themselves seriously in Davos at the World Economic Forum.

While it is common to presume that all executives need a good sense of humour, this is only part of what is required. Misused or mistimed, a joke can backfire (as the waggish Mr Blankfein found to his cost when he quipped to a reporter at the height of the banking crisis that he and Goldman Sachs were 'doing God's work').

Three other elements are essential: confidence, the right context and control.

Mr Zalm's turn as 'Priscilla, Queen of the Debt Markets' was not as surprising – or quite as outrageous – as it seemed. The ABN head is not a typical po-faced pillar of society. As Dutch finance minister, he was a jocular presence at EU meetings and he has an unconventional streak. He evidently shares with Sir Richard Branson, another confident corporate boss with a record of occasional public cross-dressing, a keen sense of what humour can achieve.

The setting was important, too. ABN's Dutch employees at the annual new year's cabaret represented a sympathetic audience, for whom this broad humour is part of a cultural tradition. It is difficult to tell how many cringed and how many cried with laughter, but they were already primed to expect something entertaining from Mr Zalm (who had played his 'brother' in previous years' skits). What they got was a lecture on values such as trust and professionalism, dressed up in a way few will forget.

Finally, control. The ABN chairman wrote his own script, and read it from the transparent autocues that politicians favour. The risky part came not when he applied his lipstick but when he opted to release the act to the rest of the world via YouTube – and even that was a calculated decision taken with the bank's press office.

Generally, executives stop clowning about as they ascend the corporate hierarchy because they become nervous about ridicule, misunderstanding and exposure. No manager who watched the UK version of *The Office* has felt quite the same about comic fancy dress at work since the episode about a charity fundraising day, in which team leader David Brent gets the news he is being made redundant and stands to reveal he is wearing a yellow ostrich costume.

Globalisation and social media, though boons for business, have severely cramped witty executives' style as they worry about wisecracks failing to cross borders or, worse, sparking a diplomatic incident en route.

But as they reach the top, executives have the licence to clown again. They should use it more frequently. Humour can have a measurable positive impact on performance. Some much-cited research from 1999[36] suggests constructive humour used by the right type of manager can prompt greater collective productivity.

Subsequent efforts to expand on this work have included some fun-wrecking attempts to give executives a template for which kinds of wittiness to deploy and when – one study features a flowchart called an 'Organisational Humour Model'.

But the only important point to remember is that an approach that works in some situations will not work in others. Self-deprecation is a great way for leaders to narrow the gap with their staff, encouraging team spirit. But if the boss is mingling with other bosses, research shows he or she is less likely to indulge in a little light *zelfspot*, for fear of losing credibility.

The World Economic Forum is said to be a place where business and political leaders feel they can let their hair down. But there is a good reason why Mr Zalm never wore his dress to Davos.[37]

Source: Hill, A. (2014) Bosses in drag can set a good tone at the top, *Financial Times*, 20 January 2014.
© The Financial Times Limited 2014. All Rights Reserved.

Leadership lessons:

1. Do not overestimate the power of bonuses and other monetary incentives: they have limited use in only limited circumstances.

2. By all means aim high, but do not forget to celebrate 'small wins', too.

3. Regular performance appraisal is valuable, but forced ranking is invidious and dangerous.

4. Do not underestimate the power of simple gratitude, sincerely spoken.

5. Businesses that follow a clear purpose perform well and attract and retain staff, but beware the slide into meaningless mission statements.

6. Never take yourself too seriously.

Making

Innovation, production and marketing are the core of what companies do. When companies say they 'make' something, the product is the combination of all three of these elements, and leaders that starve innovation, bungle production or misdirect marketing will not last long.

Theories about how to encourage innovation are confused and the practice of innovation is riven with contradictions. Invention is often mistaken for innovation. Innovation is assumed to apply only to technology, or to hardware, when the greatest innovations – think of the idea of management itself – are often new ways of doing business. Critically, innovation is misperceived as being exclusively about the production of something entirely novel. Yet it could equally consist of weaving together existing practices in new ways or mining old ideas for new situations.

Even when a great new product has emerged, manufacturing it and getting to market are fraught with risk. Leaders of innovative companies must still run an efficient production line, navigate the complexities of stretched supply chains, and tackle branding and marketing in ways that appeal widely but avoid controversy. All this needs to take place in a world where what looks right for global customers may clash with local tastes.

In one of my first attempts to tackle the subject of innovation in my column, I started with the problem of definition. What exactly *is* innovation?

The tight controls needed for creativity

By Andrew Hill

Financial Times May 30, 2011

In 2008, Samsung ran a print advertisement picturing a lissom young couple next to a forest road. They have dismounted from their mountain

➡

bikes to tend to an injured young deer. Mr Lissom has unfurled a flexible electronic display from the side of his mobile phone and is consulting a website about first aid for fawns. Samsung researchers are 'inventing new technologies one could only imagine', the copy boasts, 'so getting real-time interactive first-aid instructions for a wild animal at a moment's notice becomes a real possibility'.

I cut out the page and stuck it above my desk: a warning of what could happen if innovation were allowed to run amok.

Keeping innovation useful is a constant challenge for big companies, partly because it is so hard to pin down. Asked to pick from four definitions of innovation at London Business School's Global Leadership Summit last week, 58 per cent of the audience selected the shortest and widest (from The Economist): 'fresh thinking that creates value'. But such a broad definition could be applied not only to the technology that may give the world the mobile emergency veterinary information service it has long desired, but also to the service itself, to the way it is conceived, developed and sold, and even to the business model of the company that came up with the idea.

No wonder virtually every business with a public face includes the word 'innovation' in its mission statement, making the term as meaningless as 'shareholder value' and 'sustainability'.

Yet I still agree with the broad view laid out decades ago by management thinker Peter Drucker: that innovation is one of only two basic functions of business (the other being marketing). Without innovation, as George Buckley, chief executive of 3M, pointed out at the LBS conference, most companies would never beat a benchmark growth rate. Yet even Mr Buckley, a hard-headed Yorkshireman running a global manufacturer, says the greatest innovations benefit from a sprinkling of hard-to-define 'pixie dust'. Try putting that in a spreadsheet and determining its return on investment.

How to foster innovation is easier than deciding what it is. Academics and executives agree that freedom – including freedom to fail occasionally – is one key to creativity. Small, flexible, diverse groups of workers will generate more ideas than hidebound hierarchies. Managers should encourage staff to talk to each other and share ideas, increasingly with inventive third parties from outside the company.

They should also give reports space and remove barriers between divisions – sometimes literally. A new report out on Tuesday from Microsoft says shared workspaces and open stairwells all help encourage chance encounters that generate fresh ideas. It says GlaxoSmithKline and Philips are examples of 'hybrid organisations' that have reaped the benefits.

Finally, innovators need time. Google is known for allowing its engineers '20 per cent time' – one day a week to work on their own projects. 3M has offered its staff '15 per cent time' since 1948 (although, interestingly, it works out more like 5 per cent when staff who decline the offer are taken into account).

Applied loosely, these suggestions would be a licence for laxity. Companies need to focus. Procter & Gamble's attempt to 'systematise' innovation gets star billing in the latest Harvard Business Review.[38] Half its projects now meet profit and revenue targets, up from 15 per cent in 2000. ArcelorMittal, which boasts that innovation 'is a mindset', concentrates its $280m research and development budget on automotive steel, where it can add most value by improving the high-margin products' ability to compete against carbon-fibre or aluminium alternatives. One of the biggest challenges for chief executives and boards is to know when to kill off developers' ideas, says Martin Smith, who specialises in technology and innovation at PA Consulting.

That leaves a final problem of how to gauge what is – or will be – a success. Here consensus eludes the experts. Even Drucker framed the appraisal of innovation performance as a series of questions and admitted that it came down to 'assessment rather than measurement'.

Which gives us a final, overarching definition of innovation: the throbbing headache the chief executive takes home at the end of the day.[39]

Source: Hill, A. (2011) The tight controls needed for creativity, *Financial Times*, 30 May 2011.
© The Financial Times Limited 2011. All Rights Reserved.

Creative people are difficult to lead, as this early column hinted. A year later, a fascinating piece of research about 'creative deviance' confronted me with the first of many apparent contradictions: allowing truly creative innovators too much freedom might actually be counterproductive.

How to conform to creative deviance

By Andrew Hill

Financial Times April 30, 2012

The 1993 invention of a high-brightness, blue, light-emitting diode, which opened the way for the now-ubiquitous white LED, is often told as a tale of against-all-odds innovation by a maverick genius. When Nichia of Japan ordered researcher Shuji Nakamura[40] to stop the expensive work on the project it had initially funded, he ploughed on. He secretly sought patents for his breakthrough. He even triggered several explosions in his laboratory.

But what if the intransigence of Prof Nakamura's superiors helped to fuel his burst of radical creativity? And what if companies could harness such a force?

Babis Mainemelis, of Greece's ALBA Graduate Business School, suggests it is possible to reconcile the evidence that managers can build frameworks for creativity and the apparently contradictory finding that staff working in direct breach of managerial edicts sometimes achieve great imaginative leaps.[41] Prof Nakamura is one example of the latter, he says. Others include Francis Ford Coppola, whose film *The Godfather* 'violated Paramount's directives about plot, cast, budget and location', and Charles House of Hewlett-Packard, who defied orders from David Packard himself not to develop large-screen displays.

A new study backed by Adobe says six out of 10 adults consider themselves to be 'someone who creates', but that much of our ability to create is untapped (the survey comes up with a suspiciously precise figure of 41 per cent).[42]

Another, from FutureStep, part of recruitment company Korn/Ferry, says creativity now ranks above customer focus and strategic agility as the quality most sought-after in managers hired for long-term impact.[43] Jonah Lehrer's book *Imagine*, which explains the science of creativity, from Bob Dylan to Procter & Gamble, is topping bestseller lists.

This flowering of interest in creative people could be a signal that the recession's survivors are now refocusing on growth. It could be merely the latest reflection of a human desire to be recognised as autonomous producers of novel ideas, instead of helpless grunts, at the mercy of martinet managers at work and television tastemakers at home. It could be a sign of spring.

Whatever has triggered the appetite, corporate executives are desperate to sate it. The classic examples of creative good practice are 3M or, latterly, Google. They are regularly praised for setting aside free time for free thinking by staff. But companies could also encourage 'creative deviance', says Prof Mainemelis. Early evidence from his follow-up studies – for instance, at an advertising agency – seem to support the proposition that managers could spark deviants' imagination with a combination of tolerance, reward and, occasionally, punishment of their rule-breaking.

He admits that 'truly organising for creativity, not just celebrating it, does have some destabilising effects'. Doubtless the LED pioneer's colleagues, who came in one morning to find their lab benches scorched by his unauthorised experiments, would agree. But without the usual pressures to conform, innovations covertly developed by creative deviants stand a better chance of being radical successes, or so the theory goes.

I have three main concerns. The most trivial is that a plague of organisations will wackily restyle themselves as 'deviant-friendly', even though enshrining rule-breaking as one of the house rules seems to invite failure.

A second fear is that some clumsy managers will endorse creative flights of fancy among staff whose roles are strictly delineated for good reason – say, commercial airline pilots, accountants or surgeons. By all means, unshackle teams that design aircraft, surgical techniques or even accounting standards. But the limits on deviance must be clear. Tolerating those who creatively trespass out of bounds is one thing; turning a blind eye to others who leak commercial secrets, imperil customers' safety, or entirely neglect their day job is quite another.

Finally, I worry that the idea that leaders should be deliberately inconsistent in tackling creative deviants will set a bad precedent. Arbitrariness – singling out some employees for praise but randomly castigating others – is a cardinal management sin in my book. Still, with appropriate caveats, if it proves to be the best way to propagate a new burst of creativity, innovation and growth, it could be the exception that proves the rule.[44]

Source: Hill, A. (2012) How to conform to creative deviance, *Financial Times*, 30 April 2012.
© The Financial Times Limited 2012. All Rights Reserved.

The problem with innovation – as Peter Drucker's insight about the difficulty of appraising innovation performance suggests – is that so often success emerges from contradictory forces, sparking off each other. There are usually plenty of sparks flying at the FT's Innovate conference, which I co-chair, and every year it yields new insights into the practice of innovation. That was particularly true of the 2013 edition, which inspired this column about the importance (or otherwise) of rules for innovation.

The rules of innovation can be flexible

By Andrew Hill

Financial Times November 11, 2013

If a destination's desirability is measured by the number of maps that claim to lead you to it, innovation is the corporate world's Taj Mahal. Among the manuals on sale is an Innovator's Guide, a Cookbook, a Toolkit, a Path, a Way, a Handbook and a Manifesto.

My addition to the genre would be The Innovator's Contradictions. Insights gleaned from last week's FT Innovate conference suggest that, for almost every rule of innovation, there is an innovator who has made a breakthrough – and a fortune – flouting it. Here are seven examples.

- *Flexibility achieves more than process and structure.* 'Processes don't get people excited,' says Michel van Hove of Strategos, the consultancy. Process without purpose does indeed numb the mind, making useful, let alone innovative, work impossible. But without structure, innovators become lazy. Start-ups can be a near-perfect amalgam of purpose and process – but as soon as they get bigger, they require rules, which can even spur creativity.

- *The best innovations are conceived on a shoestring budget.* 'Frugal' innovation has many champions. But do not confuse innovative products or services for customers on a budget with low-budget innovation. Lockheed Martin's Skunk Works, which developed next-generation jet fighters, became a byword for how companies can take great leaps by developing new products secretly and away from the corporate centre. But as Luke Mansfield, European head of product innovation for Samsung Electronics, points out, the aerospace group staffed the unit with its best people and invested heavily in it.

- *Youth trumps experience.* Members of the digital generation do have an edge in appreciating and assessing the value of social and mobile innovations. But Mr Mansfield says he looks for people who have brought innovative concepts to market and, as a result, 'know when to fight and when to give up'. Companies have a habit of promoting experienced innovators into management, sacrificing their skills to the bureaucracy. He predicts they will develop innovation collectives and 'experience farms' that cultivate and share this scarce resource.

- *Innovations are always new.* By definition, yes. But often the most useful innovation is one that takes an established tool or habit and develops a new way of using or exploiting it. Klarna, a Swedish e-payment company, has found that buy-now, pay-later invoicing remains very popular. Indeed the number of customers opting for it is increasing. Klarna has duly given this venerable payment method a new platform for the internet age.

■ *Keep experimenting.* Hal Gregersen of Insead – co-author of one of the better innovation manuals, *The Innovator's DNA* – uses the example of Coinstar, the US manufacturer of machines to convert loose cash into notes, which tested customer enthusiasm for a new approach by creating cardboard replicas of machines, with real staff inside. Social media and online testing allow innovators to trial many variants of products. But they ignore at their peril the success of product-obsessives such as Apple's Steve Jobs or Lee Kun-hee, Samsung's chairman, who incinerated 150,000 defective cellphones in a field outside a factory in 1995, then ordered bulldozers to drive over them. The 'fail fast' ethos of many companies must be combined with relentless perfectionism.

■ *Loyalty breeds complacency.* It is modish to suggest you should encourage your best staff to leave – or at least not fight to keep them. But the risk is that your transient team will never be together long enough to build anything of value. Loyalty can be a competitive advantage. According to Ben Holmes, partner at venture capital group Index Ventures, this is why the hub for computer gaming innovation is in Europe, not Silicon Valley, where rivals poach skilled developers with the promise of Twitter-sized success before they can make their mark at their previous employer.

Finally, do not just assume that *innovation is about technology.* As Werner Vogels, Amazon's chief technology officer, told last week's conference, innovation is 'a business revolution, not a technology revolution'. Amazon makes a point of having neither a research and development department, nor a vice-president of innovation. Everyone must come up with new business ideas. Innovation is about people. If you can persuade your staff it is not always synonymous with pure science or gorgeous gadgetry, that really will be a breakthrough.[45]

Source: Hill, A. (2013) The rules of innovation can be flexible, *Financial Times*, 11 November 2013.
© The Financial Times Limited 2013. All Rights Reserved.

No passage on innovation is complete these days without a reference to Apple, which seems to have mastered all the elements from innovation, via design, to production and marketing of its products, creating its own cluster of innovation among its suppliers in the process. Recent history is littered with companies that were not sufficiently innovative to keep up – Nokia, BlackBerry, even Sony, the company that Jobs himself most admired.

The next column appeared just after the 2015 launch of the Apple Watch. It remains to be seen whether my judgement of the limited utility of the Apple Watch stands the test of time – more recent reviews suggest perception of its usefulness improves with wearing. But I think the conclusion that you do not always have to flee the jungle clearing when the 800-pound gorilla arrives will remain valid.

Apple Watch shows the strategic ripple effects of a big splash

By Andrew Hill

Financial Times March 16, 2015

Whenever chief executives babble about 'ecosystems' – as they often do – I picture one of those school biology diagrams of a pond: bacteria at the bottom, algae floating on top, and maybe a stickleback or two darting about below the surface.

Occasionally, a bigger fish dives in. That is what chief executive Tim Cook did last week when he launched the Apple Watch. As the ripples fan out, other pond-dwellers now have a choice: adapt, struggle along, or look for another habitat.

First to rise from the sludge at the bottom were China's counterfeiters, who were brazenly advertising knock-offs of the new device before Mr Cook had drawn breath. Once the watch itself hits the market, or Apple's lawyers hit them in the courts, many are likely to sink back into the mud. The bigger question is for legitimate traders. The watch's arrival could shake up many product categories, from luxury goods and fitness accessories to, well, watches.

How should you react if a powerful new product looms into sight in your sector? Even for companies outside technology and wearables, the lessons of previous Apple launches still apply.

Ask yourself first how revolutionary the new gadget is.

The watch is unusual for Apple. It is a shiny pendant to the iPhone, rather than a substitute (the iPhone, by contrast, reduced the best-selling iPod to an app). But Scott Anthony, author of *The First Mile*, about how to bring ideas to market, says that if a new entrant aims to do the same job your product does, does the job as well or better than yours, and is at least as simple to use, you have a problem.

In assessing new rivals, though, do not take too narrow a view of the new device. Nokia stumbled in 2007 partly because it treated the newly launched iPhone merely as a phone – one that was less useful, less sophisticated and more fragile (Nokia engineers noted disdainfully that it had failed its 'drop test')[46] than its existing best-selling models.

Similarly, an over-simplistic view of the Apple Watch may underestimate how it could meet previously unremarked needs, excite users merely through its superior design, or channel them to other new products and services, just as the iPhone encouraged the growth of iTunes and the App Store.

If you decide you must react, be decisive. Google's Android switched course to meet the iPhone touchscreen challenge as soon as the new phone appeared. One Android engineer, quoted by Fred Vogelstein in his book *Battle of the Titans*, about the Apple-Google rivalry, commented: 'What we had suddenly looked just so . . . nineties.'[47] On the other hand, when Verizon Wireless asked BlackBerry to devise an 'iPhone killer',[48] it took too long to produce the Storm touchscreen phone, which was buggy and disliked. Verizon ultimately turned to Google's Motorola and Android combination for an alternative.

One possibility is simply to pull out of the market altogether. A former technology chief executive told me recently that his team was in the latter stages of developing a touchscreen tablet when Apple launched the iPad in 2010. Despite the sunk cost, he scrapped the project after realising Apple's version was simply better in all respects. But competing in the tablet market was not critical to the future of his company in the way smartphones were vital to BlackBerry or Nokia. For them, ignoring Apple was simply not an option.

For smaller companies, though, it may ultimately be more profitable to wait and see. Anindya Ghose, professor of IT and marketing at New York University's Stern School, says: 'When Apple makes such a big splash, whether it sells or not, it creates an awareness about a gadget of this kind.'

Pebble, the crowdfunded watchmaker that already offers a number of popular, less expensive alternatives to the Apple Watch, styles itself as the incumbent to beat. But it is more likely to prosper by dominating another part of the larger market opened up by Apple, just as smaller retailers benefit from traffic to the mall when an 'anchor tenant' such as a big department store leases space.

My pond analogy is too restrictive, in other words. New and heavily marketed products open up space for others to thrive. As an alternative to being swamped, positioning yourself to catch the wave from a big new arrival's splash could be good business. For those hanging back, this could even be the moment to take the plunge.[49]

Source: Hill, A. (2015) Apple Watch shows the strategic ripple effects of a big splash, *Financial Times*, 16 March 2015.
© The Financial Times Limited 2015. All Rights Reserved.

What distinguishes innovation from pure research is the ability – in fact, the necessity – to produce, market and sell the product. Technological innovations such as 3D printing, better described as additive manufacturing, are now shaking up production processes. But the real revolutions in manufacturing are revolutions of process rather than technology and, after Henry Ford, Eiji Toyoda deserves a place in the Hall of Fame of innovative production pioneers.

Toyoda's legacy goes well beyond the lean

By Andrew Hill

Financial Times September 30, 2013

Eiji Toyoda was the man who taught the world's production workers Japanese. If you know *kaizen* means continuous improvement, and use *kanban* inventory tags to eliminate *muda*, or waste, then Toyoda, who died recently, was your *sensei*.

The Toyota Production System he championed as head of the carmaker in the 1970s and 1980s, traces its roots to a fail-safe device devised by Toyoda's uncle to cope with thread breaks on mechanical looms.

Multinationals have since turned its efficiency methods – 'lean' production, just-in-time supply chains and outsourcing – into a habit that is woven through the fabric of global production. However, in future, Toyoda's insights into the power of human initiative will be more relevant.

Modern manufacturing is moving, using 3D printing and other methods, through mass customisation of small batches to affordable personalisation of individual items. Crowd and cloud are unpicking the production lines Toyoda revolutionised, while manufacturers look to make more money from services than products.

TPS is still 'the dominant design in high volume manufacturing', according to Willy Shih of Harvard Business School, who puts Toyoda in the management pantheon alongside Henry Ford. His system is already capable of producing millions of product variants. In *The New Industrial Revolution*, my former *Financial Times* colleague Peter Marsh estimates that across the Toyota range 'in the course of a year's output . . . a maximum of only about five [vehicles] share the same product features'.

But companies will increasingly have to recognise, learn and apply more of TPS's core people management principles, some of which have been obscured by an obsession with 'leanness'.

Lean production has given TPS a bad name, by associating it with cost reduction and job cuts. Yet people were always at its centre. Taiichi Ohno,[50] Toyoda's chief production engineer, called it 'autonomation' – or 'automation with a human touch'. Ohno gave the lie to the idea that people management was a 'soft skill'; he was like an 'authoritarian schoolmaster', according to one account. However, he insisted teams should work out how to solve problems on the line themselves. That philosophy of respect was passed on. When Toyota sought to teach its practices to US suppliers in the early 1990s, it was a precondition that they should redeploy displaced production line workers.

Manufacturing expert Lord Bhattacharyya of the University of Warwick says Toyota's experts saw inventory reduction as simple common sense – born of necessity in resource- and space-constrained Japan after the Second World War. He says consultants hyped 'leanness' to their clients, peddling production-line efficiency to the exclusion of all else, to the irritation of keepers of Toyoda's flame.

One of those guardians – Jeff Liker, professor of industrial and operations engineering at the University of Michigan and author of *The Toyota Way* – says all but a few organisations that use the Toyota system are 'scratching the surface' of its deeper benefits.

As computerised production becomes more sophisticated, companies will have to place greater faith in an ever more skilled workforce. To flourish, they will need, in Prof Liker's words, to become 'learning organisations, constantly adapting to [their] environment'. As such, they will be direct heirs to Toyoda and Ohno, whose hard-nosed perfectionism was built on an appetite for learning, whetted on visits to sprawling US car plants and abundantly stocked supermarkets in the 1950s.

Toyoda's production practices will not disappear. A system for simplifying complex manufacturing and supply chain challenges remains useful. You will continue to find *kanban* and *kaizen* from Shenzhen to Sheffield. But the change he inspired in the culture of manufacturing was far more profound. It will also prove to be far more enduring and relevant for modern businesses, whether their staff work in a single factory, are dispersed up and down the global value chain, or form a collaborative open network of freelancers.

So set aside the paraphernalia of lean production for a moment. It is only the most visible of Eiji Toyoda's legacies. He insisted, above all, that managers should listen to the people who design, build and make things, and reward them for improvements they suggested. That is a language everyone should learn.[51]

Source: Hill, A. (2013) Toyoda's legacy goes well beyond the lean, *Financial Times*, 30 September 2013.
© The Financial Times Limited 2013. All Rights Reserved.

Without salespeople, the best innovation and the leanest production could be worthless. I started with some personal cynicism about the sales function, and plenty of preconceptions about how it might be affected by the world of ecommerce.

I think leaders of big companies selling to retail customers will increasingly start to mimic supermarket chiefs, who, because of the sheer number and variety of items that they turn over, have come to depend more on data, gleaned through loyalty cards and other means, and to rely on combinations of services to encourage customer loyalty. Justin King, when chief executive of J Sainsbury, the UK retailer, called these 'points of Velcro', one example being the way supermarkets have added banking services or offered 'click-and-collect' depots that encourage customers to pick up another item or two while in the store.

But I found, from personal experience as well as further research, that there is still a place for old-fashioned sales techniques.

The web has not yet killed the art of sales

By Andrew Hill

Financial Times December 2, 2013

Call me naive, but somehow I expected more from the double-glazing salesman I recently invited into my home. I knew about confusing pitches, pressure tactics, cowboy installers and fly-by-night manufacturers. You do not have to do much research to appreciate that sellers of double glazing are in the hard-sell hall of fame, alongside used-car vendors and estate agents.

But I had also read the latest literature – such as Dan Pink's book *To Sell Is Human* – which points to a change in the selling culture. The internet has evened up the odds.

Customers are now as well, if not better, informed than sales agents. I needed new windows and I reckoned I would at least gain an insight into a more transparent era of selling.

I reckoned wrong. The national company I asked to quote first sent an old-school salesman with a box of all the worn-out tricks I thought the web was supposed to have eliminated: the 'limited availability' discount; the sign-now, pay-less offer; and the 'why wouldn't you?' financing deal. He insisted I should sign up to the last, even after I had mentioned I worked for the FT and wanted more time to examine the terms. Until I made clear a local supplier had got the job, the company kept harassing me with follow-up calls.

Why have these techniques survived? In part, because of the nature of the product. In all except newly built homes, windows are non-standard, tailored to the size and condition of the hole they fill. Online double-glazing companies do exist, but the choices, befuddling jargon (espangolet or shootbolt locking?), and risk of getting the order expensively wrong, would drive even dedicated bargain hunters back to a more old-fashioned intermediary.

Life is harder for sales forces in other areas. Take another bespoke glazed item – prescription spectacles.

Giving a cruel twist to the competitive challenge, online rivals prosper in part because incumbent opticians carry out the all-important eye tests for them. Armed with this information – equivalent to my window measurements – customers order lenses with relative confidence online, while browsing limitless options for frames. The cost of going wrong is low. Opticians are left fighting a rearguard action based on limited stock, sketchy personal service and customers' residual fears about trusting their vision to an anonymous website.

Online competition and comparison have turned mobile phone purchase on its head, too. Phone contracts in the UK are notoriously complex. Yet as a sales tactic, obfuscation has its limits these days. When I upgraded my phone recently, I had a clear idea of the model I wanted and the package of voice, data and texts I needed. Unable to cut her price, the nice saleswoman at my existing operator was powerless to prevent my switching to a competitor, whose offer I could see online while I negotiated.

The notion that in this tougher environment most sales teams are at best weakened and at worst redundant is not as compelling as it may look, however. Mr Pink says the data show salespeople are still 'a stalwart part of labour markets around the world'. But to survive, they have to learn to 'upserve' customers rather than simply upsell to them. He cites companies such as Microchip Technology, a US semiconductor company, which decreased the variable element of its vendors' pay, and saw sales rise.

Apple hires brand converts for its stores because, as FT contributor Philip Delves Broughton has written, they sell 'out of enthusiasm, not just for commission'.[52]

My unpleasant encounter with old style sales was, in some ways, rather reassuring. Techniques have not changed as much as some evangelists claim. The human touch remains vital. The way my double glazing salesman got me to provide clues about myself as he ran through his patter was impressive, even if he then went on to ignore them.

But while I suspect it will take time for online competition to smash double glazing, sales agents who focus narrowly on closing the deal could still benefit from a wider perspective, as a final personal sales tale suggests. Facing a big bill to repair our ageing people-carrier, I consulted a former car salesman, recommended by a friend, who now helps buyers navigate the used car market. Should we repair or replace the vehicle, I asked, expecting a self-interested response. He suggested repair. Guess who is the first person I will call when replacement becomes our only option.[53]

Source: Hill, A. (2013) The web has not yet killed the art of sales, *Financial Times*, 2 December 2013.
© The Financial Times Limited 2013. All Rights Reserved.

Finally, companies are in a constant battle to keep their innovative flame alight, against the pressure to commoditise the product. The coincidence, in 2015, of two private equity deals – one a sale, the other a purchase – allowed me to make an unusual parallel.

Contortions are required for Cirque du Soleil to keep its magic

By Andrew Hill

Financial Times April 27, 2015

When it comes to management challenges, fish fingers and circuses are at opposite extremes: one product is the acme of industrialised food processing, the other the ultimate expression of human creativity and energy. Somehow, private equity has found room for both: last week, Permira agreed to sell Iglo, which makes Birds Eye fish fingers in Europe, after nine years running the frozen foods company, while another buyout group, TPG Capital, led a deal to gain control of Montreal's Cirque du Soleil.

The coincidence made me wonder at the sheer breadth of private equity-owned businesses, which seems to defy the caricature of buyout kings as asset-stripping short-termists, interested only in targets with an annuity-like stream of revenue. But something else links these two apparently disparate businesses. All great enterprises start like a troupe of inventive and inspired circus performers. But over time most end up churning out the equivalent of pre-cut breaded strips of reconstituted seafood. The big question is: how can entrepreneurial and inventive companies slow their slippery slide to a fish-fingery fate?

I do not mean to disparage the creativity involved in food production. Iglo's new owner, Nomad Foods, says innovation is one reason it is ready to pay €2.6bn. A few years ago, when I visited Birds Eye's plant in Lowestoft, on England's easternmost tip, the man in charge would not let the FT photograph his state of the art potato-waffle-packer, he was justly proud of the scanners that screen out dodgy-coloured peas before processing, and he was trialling new ready-meal combinations. But such incremental innovations are a long way from the original breakthrough of the eccentric Clarence Birdseye,[54] who in the early 20th century, inspired by how Inuit people preserved the fish they

➡

caught, invented a way of processing flash-frozen food in bulk and thus launched a billion microwave television suppers.

Birds Eye sold out to the Post food empire and Goldman Sachs in 1929. It is hard to tell whether it was a critical turning point in how the business was managed. The founder was always interested in mass manufacturing and continued his innovative research. But the parallel with the dilemma that has faced Cirque du Soleil co-founder Guy Laliberté is intriguing and instructive.

Mr Laliberté wanted to keep control. He plays a lead role in management case studies, from *Blue Ocean Strategy* to Harvard Business School, based on how he and colleagues revived the tired circus format in the 1980s, with a new spectacle based on human skills and theatricality. He has long employed outside directors for the shows, but has a strong say in what they produce.

When you are the creative driving force and majority owner of any business, all interests are aligned. Mr Laliberté will stay involved after the sale. But the fear is that Cirque has taken a step down the tightrope that leads to mere mass production. Ajay Agrawal of Toronto's Rotman management school points out that once 90 per cent of the company has passed to TPG and other outside shareholders, 'you can imagine a world where he says "I think we should do this creative show" and the people who stand to make a financial gain or loss say "that's too risky"'.

Daniel Lamarre, Cirque's chief executive, denies that will happen. He told me the buyers understood they 'could spend a lot of time looking at the numbers but if the creativity is not there . . . you are losing everything'.

Four things have to happen to keep that aim alive. The new owners must let the group's directors take artistic risks or there will be no business. The creative team must let the owners take steps to ensure Cirque's commercial health, or there will be no art. The managers themselves bear a bigger responsibility now to mediate between owners and artists. All must ensure that the owners honour undertakings to keep Cirque rooted in Montreal, where it has seeded an innovative cluster of some 40 circus companies.

Calculated risk-taking, commercial stability, management skill and a sense of history: these are prerequisites to stop innovative businesses turning into mere same-again production lines. Patrick Leroux of Montreal's Concordia University, who studies circus culture, says Cirque's new owners and their agents in management 'have to focus on research and development and the creative core: otherwise it will just be a brand'. A bit like Birds Eye, in fact, only with contortionists on the payroll not fish-packers.[55]

FT

Source: Hill, A. (2015) Contortions are required for Cirque du Soleil to keep its magic, *Financial Times*, 27 April 2015.
© The Financial Times Limited 2015. All Rights Reserved.

Leadership lessons:

1. The 'rules' of innovation are often contradictory – so be careful not to follow the rules too slavishly.

2. Time and freedom are keys to encouraging innovation and creativity . . .

3. . . . but sometimes innovators need to be constrained.

4. Stay open to change and ideas from outside.

5. Combine innovation with effective production, sales and marketing.

6. Get your creatives to work constructively with their commercial counterparts.

7. Stay alert to the possibility that today's breakthrough product is tomorrow's fish finger.

Shaping

Whether you find, inherit, build or are handed a business to run, you must shape it. Perhaps the business already has a strong corporate culture, but one not adapted to the times. Possibly the organisation has gone bad and needs to be changed. Or maybe the company you run and the people who work for it need to be reformed and sharpened to take on new challenges.

In any case, a leader needs to shape his or her team. Jack Welch, former chief executive of General Electric, used to say that the most important part of his important job was to hire good people – people who were smarter than him. But leaders also need to inspire their teams to work in the right way, to behave with integrity, and to acquire the skills to shape their own teams.

Many studies confirm that a diverse team – by which I mean a team whose members think in different ways, not just one of mixed gender or ethnicity – performs better than one that is homogeneous. But such teams are also harder to manage, even assuming you can assemble them in the first place, given the need to have certain functional skills represented.

Talking of GE, I was struck by the range of traits that Jeffrey Immelt, Jack Welch's successor as chief executive, now expects his lieutenants to demonstrate (some enumerated in the column below), and to combine with deep specialist knowledge of areas of the conglomerate's activities. For me, it raises the question of whether anyone will ever have the rare mix of both depth and breadth to run a company of GE's size.

An all-rounder may not be the right fit

By Andrew Hill

Financial Times December 3, 2012

Ian Livingston, chief executive of BT, told me last week more than a third of the telecoms group's staff are now engineers – a higher proportion than ever. But whereas their expertise once covered mainly the maintenance and repair of an analogue telephone network, he now expects them to do more.

At BT, the ideal field employee – who used to need 'craft and mechanical skills', according to another executive – must combine in-depth expertise in a particular domain with broad knowledge of other areas.

But while the drive to employ such 'T-shaped' workers makes sense, it also makes me anxious – and not only because I think of myself as a generalist journalist, another category doomed to extinction.

Specialist skills are in high demand, particularly in fast-growing economies. McKinsey reports that the number of highly educated workers needed by 2020 in China and Brazil could exceed supply (by 23m, in China's case).[56] Attempts to fill these gaps could create a generation of narrow experts. It will fall to companies to improve their staff's breadth of knowledge through training, while workers will have to be as adaptable as possible.

To respond to these contradictory pressures, big employers need to know what skills are required for the future and whether the experts who can help reach those goals already work for the company.

Alcatel-Lucent, for instance, has an internal job market to ensure the telecoms equipment group capitalises on employees' existing skills. Such initiatives help retain staff and cut the cost and risk of recruiting externally. But it is easier to put specialists on the front line and give them the flexibility to work across different disciplines than it is to find senior managers who strike the perfect balance of breadth and depth.

Companies obviously believe such paragons exist. Barclays implies Antony Jenkins was picked as chief executive because, despite a career in retail banking, he is a 'T-shaped man', able to understand the priorities of the whole group. Singapore is basing the next phase of its economic growth in part on development of T-shaped professionals and executives, who possess 'both deep skills in their area of expertise and broad knowledge of horizontal skills'. General Electric wants its leaders to demonstrate expertise, but also such attributes as external focus, clear thinking, imagination and courage. By definition, if they aspire to lead GE itself, they will also need to know enough to interrogate in-house experts in jet engine technology and mortgage markets.

Recruiters naturally love to hire all-rounders. If your new finance director also speaks four languages, has a law degree and Asian experience, so much the better.

But here is where I start to worry. First, not all all-rounders are as rounded as companies may believe. If you urgently need to fill a post in finance, don't assume that the new CFO's previous experience will necessarily equip her later to run Shanghai or become general counsel.

Second, in aiming for perfect balance, employers risk crucifying senior staff on the very T-shape they want them to adopt, ending up with leaders who are neither broad enough nor deep enough. Adding to the stress, these team leaders are spread more thinly than they used to be. One reason the proportion of BT engineers has risen is that Mr Livingston has cut more deeply into the group's managerial staff.

The definition of a T-shaped manager has also become rather confused. Morten Hansen and Bolko von Oetinger used the term in 2001 to describe executives who collaborated by 'breaking out of the traditional corporate hierarchy to share knowledge freely across the organisation'.[57] But as the goals set out by Barclays, GE and the Singapore government suggest, the term now defines leaders with a wide range of capabilities.

Prof Hansen tells me he counsels companies not to assume executives have to be good at everything: 'You have to have an area of expertise and bring that to the table – otherwise you are just a facilitator – but at the same time you need to know enough about other skill areas so you can collaborate with others.'

The goal remains a good one. But some companies must start considering how far they can safely ask senior managers to stretch. As the complexities of running big organisations multiply, a few may become too broad for even the most T-shaped executives to embrace.[58]

Source: Hill, A. (2012) An all-rounder may not be the right fit, *Financial Times*, 3 December 2012.
© The Financial Times Limited 2012. All Rights Reserved.

Any discussion of teams inevitably returns to parallels in sport. When Kevin Pietersen, the mercurial and outspoken England cricketer, was dropped from the national team in 2012, it started a wider debate about whether the selectors were right. I used to believe that it was better to run a harmonious team of above-average performers than a group of *galácticos*, to use the Spanish term for the team of star footballers expensively assembled by Real Madrid in the 2000s, who (like Real Madrid in that era) may disappoint. But the abundant research on teams provides some surprising answers.

The right number of stars for a team

By Andrew Hill

Financial Times August 20, 2012

Anyone who has worked with a prima donna – and hasn't everyone? – should study the latest career moves of Kevin Pietersen and Robin van Persie.

Cricketer Pietersen, one of England's best ever batsmen, was dropped from the team last week, accused of sending what the South African-born player admitted were 'provocative' texts to the opposing South African team, allegedly denigrating the England captain. Footballer van Persie, Arsenal's captain, was sold to newly listed Manchester United, six weeks after stating on his website that he and the London club's management 'disagree on the way Arsenal FC should move forward'.

The week after a London Olympics justly celebrated for displays of team loyalty, the two men risk looking like the anti-Olympians. They probably won't care. Pietersen's skills are much in demand in the commercially driven and highly popular Indian Premier League; van Persie stands to receive up to £200,000 a week, directly and indirectly, having signed for Manchester United. However, their cases sum up a dilemma for team leaders everywhere: how hard should they strive to keep star players, and when should they let them go?

The temptation is to seek a definitive black or white answer. For example, it is a staple assumption of sports journalism that dissent in the dressing room leads to disaster on the pitch. This is not necessarily true, however – whether in sport, business or any other domain.

Richard Hackman, a Harvard psychologist who has studied symphony orchestras,[59] found that 'grumpy orchestras played together slightly better than orchestras in which all the musicians were quite happy', because, as he told the Harvard Business Review, 'when we're productive and we've done something good together . . . we feel satisfied, not the other way around'. The presumption that harmony is all-important can even undermine performance if talented team members 'self-censor their contributions' to keep the peace.

The assumption that a team full of overachieving stars will perform best also turns out to be unfounded, however. A study by Harvard

Business School's Boris Groysberg and others looked at sell-side equity analysts[60] and found that the results of the leading research teams started to wane when the proportion of stars rose above a certain level – broadly, the point at which preening individuals' selfishness and their clamour for more pay impinge on the whole team's results. 'Don't overspend to recruit high-status employees,' concludes this research – a warning perhaps van Persie's new employer should have absorbed.

Mark de Rond of Cambridge's Judge Business School points out that stars often work well in a supportive network of competent performers. As he told me: 'People are willing to put up with prima donnas, provided they get a return on [the stars'] performance.'

In his new book *There Is an I in Team*, which draws on examples of teams from sport and business, Prof de Rond writes that the best are the product of difficult trade-offs between members' 'likeability and competence . . . camaraderie and rivalry'. These tensions may be healthy, but that doesn't mean they don't feel awkward, he says. In other words, finding and then managing successfully the optimal mix of stars and team players is not easy. In fact, it is probably harder in business – where the goals are many and the routes to them varied – than in sport, where the goal is clear and team members' efforts, and results, are easy to observe and measure.

As for van Persie and Pietersen, Arsenal and England should be able to embrace such outsize talents. But the two cases are different – and not just because the Dutch striker is easier to like. 'Nobody is angry at me, I'm not angry at them', van Persie said of his parting from Arsenal, and, short-term fan anger apart, it seems to be true. His is just the latest episode in the constant (if expensive) remaking of leading football teams, whose managers, like their business counterparts, strive to balance the benefits of continuity against the advantages of renewal.

Pietersen's rift with England, by contrast, has a more serious cause that will be harder to forgive.[61] As his captain said, the differences with the batsman weren't just about his rogue texting, but related to 'a broader issue about trust and respect'. When trust in stars breaks down, it is often impossible for the rest of the team to reform around them.[62]

Source: Hill, A. (2012) The right number of stars for a team, *Financial Times*, 20 August 2012.
© The Financial Times Limited 2012. All Rights Reserved.

Teams are only one variable in the elements that leaders have to shape. The business model of your organisation may be less fungible – but the financial crisis left many thinking that there must be a problem with the dominant model of the public limited company. I begged to differ.

It's the managers, not the model

By Andrew Hill

Financial Times May 9, 2011

Tom Glocer has been celebrating the success of the three-year integration process that melded Thomson with Reuters. But the chief executive of the information and media group needs to beware overstating the value of its ownership model. In a recent *Financial Times* interview,[63] he said that Thomson Reuters – 55 per cent of which belongs to a family investment company – had 'what may become the defining corporate structure of the best institutions for the next 20 years'.

That big claim worries me. Few families are content to share their birthright with outside shareholders in a listed hybrid for long. More important, anyone who trusts specific corporate structures to do the job managers are paid to do is likely to be disappointed, or worse.

I get the same queasy feeling whenever I hear British politicians celebrate the John Lewis Partnership – the successful employee-owned department store chain – as a model for everything from the Post Office to the National Health Service. In a similar vein, the financial crisis has encouraged a think-tank fetish for proposing mutual, co-operative or partnership alternatives to the listed-company model used by broken retail or investment banks.[64]

The urge to replace the corporate tools used by bad workmen is not surprising, and nothing new. Many blame the fate of Northern Rock – the UK bank that suffered a run on deposits in 2007 and was later nationalised – on its earlier 'demutualisation' and listing. Similarly, John Micklethwait and Adrian Wooldridge recount in *The Company*, their engaging history of the joint-stock model, how the 1866 collapse of Overend, Gurney, a listed bank, prompted one critic to describe limited-liability status as 'a snare and a delusion, like the candle to the moth, or gunpowder in the hands of children'.

Primed with poorly thought-out bonuses and kindled with speculative short-term shareholdings, listed company status can be explosive. But it needs people to light the touchpaper, and incompetent or unprincipled managers can blight a mutual or a partnership as surely as they can lead a quoted company to the brink.

Britain's mutually owned building societies may be structurally conservative, but their shape did not prevent several straying into unwise property lending in the early 2000s, from which they had to be rescued by larger peers. One big society – the Dunfermline – collapsed altogether. Defenders of the mutual model argue that these enterprises were doomed simply because they diverged from the sacred mutual ethos. But Andrew Bailey, the senior Bank of England official who worked on salvaging assets from the Dunfermline wreckage, told the Building Societies Association last week that the way in which mutuals coped with the extraordinary pressure on their model during the credit boom depended on three factors: capital, funding and 'the quality of governance and management'.

Mismanagement can negate the benefits of any corporate model. United Airlines, a flagship for employee ownership when staff took a 55 per cent stake in 1995, crumbled into bankruptcy protection seven years later after rifts opened between managers and employees. In the absence of good, professional management, Spain's cajas – local savings banks that used to embody the spirit of community banking – fell under the influence of venal regional politicians and binged on property loans. Is there pressure for the *'re-caja-ización'* of these vehicles, as there is in the UK for the remutualisation of Northern Rock? *Al contrario.* The regulator is forcing them to merge with each other. Most will seek shelter – and much-needed funding – under a different model, either as quoted companies or in private equity ownership.

This is no paean for the publicly listed company, whose flaws have recently been all too evident. Mutuals, co-ops, family companies and even Thomson Reuters' family/ listed cross-breed (if Mr Glocer does his job well) can complement the quoted company structure that was the market's darling until 2007–08. Such diversity is valuable and worth nurturing. But to argue that one vehicle for business activity is inherently better than another is a little like saying a four-wheel-drive is always safer and faster than a tandem. Whether it conveys its occupants securely and speedily to their destination surely depends on who is steering it.[65]

FT   *Source:* Hill, A. (2011) It's the managers, not the model, *Financial Times*, 9 May 2011.
© The Financial Times Limited 2011. All Rights Reserved.

That column prompted a number of letters from FT readers, of which the most interesting came from David Erdal, a champion of the employee-ownership model. He took issue with what he saw as an attack on mutual or staff-owned companies, borrowing my analogy to point out that 'there are good and bad drivers – but there are also vehicles that offer their passengers considerably more protection and performance than others'.[66]

Every growing business, however constituted, needs to avoid sprawling out of control. There are plenty of ways in which leaders are encouraged to grow (some of which I address in the next chapter). But it is far harder to stop doing things.

Killing projects is the hardest innovation

By Andrew Hill

Financial Times April 1, 2013

Pascal Soriot, AstraZeneca's new chief executive, has just laid out a new strategy to 'focus, accelerate and transform' the pharmaceutical company. Mark Thompson, newly arrived at the helm of The New York Times Company, has promised to 'concentrate [the group's] strategic focus' on the core business, putting The Boston Globe up for sale and rebranding the venerable International Herald Tribune.

'Focus' is classic CEO jargon. It sounds precise and purposeful. But by implying that activities on the periphery will fade away with a twist of the strategic lens, it severely understates the struggle involved in persuading any company to stop doing certain things, and the pain of carrying out such decisions.

Good luck to Mr Soriot and Mr Thompson, but the chief problem they face is that decisions on what to give up are too often one-off dramas staged by a new boss. Instead, companies should turn their reassessment of priorities into a habit. Peter Drucker, the late management writer, called this 'systematic abandonment'. It is as vital to corporate health as systematic innovation.

Why is it so hard for companies to kill off projects? Many leaders think it is more courageous to advance, expand and acquire than to retreat, shrink and divest. At a recent strategy meeting I attended, executives' warm enthusiasm for new ventures was inversely proportional to the chill and doublespeak that filled the room when they were challenged to take the axe to longstanding initiatives.

Yet when organisations stop to scrutinise themselves, the accretion of unheeded strategy visions they find hanging around them is extraordinary.

Business leaders appointed to help oversee branches of the British civil service reported last year that some government departments had set themselves more than 60 'priorities'. But long-established bureaucracies are not alone in this. In his book *Good Strategy/ Bad Strategy*, Richard Rumelt recalls how, in the early 1990s, Digital Equipment Corporation was doomed to irrelevance because its leaders 'avoided the hard work of choice, set nothing aside, hurt no interest groups or individual egos, but crippled the whole'.

Short of a crisis – when the flames of a burning platform are licking around the boardroom – it is too easy to try to muddle through.

Corporate leaders' fear of ridicule for scuppering ventures they once launched deters them. Historic attachments, sometimes compounded by familial or cultural ties, contribute to the problem.

One CEO told me recently about a high-profile deal that foundered because the seller insisted on retaining ownership of a factory where his great-grandfather had been born. That is extreme. But residual sentimentality helps explain Rupert Murdoch's reluctance until recently to split News Corp's newspapers, the legacy of his father's original Australian business, from the empire's film and television assets. Time Warner's sluggishness in spinning off its deep-rooted Time Inc magazines division looks like another example. By contrast, I admire François-Henri Pinault's decision, having recast PPR as a luxury and sportswear company by selling retail interests it had bought, to rebrand it as Kering, not Pinault. The move symbolically distances the group from the family enterprise on which it was founded.

Companies such as Cisco or Google have become famous for serial acquisitions or constant innovation. They also need to go beyond calls for focus and build a reputation for successfully pruning unneeded projects. Both John Chambers at Cisco and Larry Page at Google have used the F-word to urge their staff to be more choosy. Consequences include the closure in 2011 of Cisco's popular Flip video camera operation and the abolition of Google Reader as part of a 'spring cleaning'.

Google was slated for that recent decision by fans of the news tool, but Mr Page's instinct is right and the metaphor is a good one. Drucker used to tell CEOs to ask themselves: 'If we did not do this already, would we

➡

go into it now?' It would be a good discipline to pose that question at least annually, just as people in colder climates traditionally dust and declutter their homes. Clearing outdated priorities and projects from the corporate attic is hard. But when the alternative is slow suffocation under the detritus of past strategic plans, it really is the only choice.[67]

Source: Hill, A. (2013) Killing projects is the hardest innovation, *Financial Times*, 1 April 2013.
© The Financial Times Limited 2013. All Rights Reserved.

Interestingly, having imposed some focus, Mr Page has since decided that Google requires a new structure in order to accommodate the ambitious long-term businesses that it still cultivates alongside its core search operation. In August 2015, he announced the foundation of Alphabet, as a new parent company for what many now characterise as a sort of technology conglomerate. For many investors, what his move may eventually presage is a break-up or spin-off of some of Google's component parts. As I wrote some years earlier, there should be no shame in that.

Breaking up is not a sign of failure

By Andrew Hill

Financial Times January 24, 2011

Three characteristics unite modern conglomerates: they abhor the conglomerate label; they rarely acknowledge the need to change shape until they decide to do so; and they never admit that external pressure prompted their break-up.

ITT used to be one reason conglomerates were shy of the title. During the 1970s, Harold Geneen built a company with 2,000 business units, from Sheraton to Wonder Bread. He preferred to call ITT a 'unified-management, multi-product company'. But in his 1984 book *Managing*, he wrote: 'I would like to think that the public has come to appreciate that a conglomerate, per se, is not an offence in nature.'

Fat chance. Geneen, for all his skills, added to suspicion about conglomerates. It hardly helped that his ITT was accused of bribery, complicity with the CIA (in undermining Salvador Allende, president of Chile) and lack of accountability. His successor, Rand Araskog broke ITT up in 1995, conceding later that he should have done it 10 years before, when corporate raiders first attacked the multi-product mammoth.

Now, ITT is again splitting itself three ways, to investors' delight. Demergers are in vogue: Marathon Oil, Fortune Brands and Fiat have all spun parts of themselves off, or plan to. British 'multi-industry company' Smiths Group is under pressure to sell businesses. General Electric is concentrating on its industrial operations.

But although focus is in and sprawl is out, the conglomerate still has its time and its place. In fast-growth countries, that time is now. As Tarun Khanna and Krishna Palepu point out in their 2010 book *Winning in Emerging Markets*, where institutional voids exist – as in, say, India – conglomerates, often family-controlled, can fill the vacuum. They move capital and people internally instead of relying on scant or non-existent external financial or human resources.

In developed markets like the US, United Technologies, Danaher – and even GE – continue to champion diversification.

Large private equity funds look like conglomerates, though an unfortunate appetite for leverage has temporarily obscured their main virtue: an ability to manage diverse operations more directly – and with fewer distractions – than listed company shareholders can.

So the question is not how soon the model will disappear – it won't. The question is how to manage a conglomerate and, equally important, how to decide when its time is up.

On the public markets, this question lies behind fund managers' assertions that they could assemble a portfolio of single-sector companies, each well run, instead of owning a conglomerate that trades at a discount to the sum of its parts.

Steve Loranger, chief executive of the modern ITT, faced an easier decision than his predecessors: US government budget cuts made it obvious the group's defence equipment business was holding back the shares. But few emperors time their empire's break-up well. Most have to feel activist shareholders' hot breath on their necks before they yield. Even Mr Loranger had faced investor threats to shake up the board.

Still, it is human nature for leaders to want to emulate corporate titans, feted for managing vast corporate dominions. Andrew Campbell of the Ashridge Strategic Management Centre likens bosses' resistance to communist leaders' stubbornness as the Soviet bloc disintegrated.

Ed Breen, who led Tyco into a three-way break-up in 2007 and still runs the industrial arm, told me: 'You've got to take your ego out of the conversation and ask: what's best for the business?' Instead, some leaders can turn from masters of management to masters of self-justification, publicly hailing the benefits of breadth and scale right until the moment they convert to the cult of focus and specialisation.

It makes more sense to keep the structure under constant scrutiny. Compared with the glory of a big merger, selling once-core operations or splitting the business up seems humdrum. But such deals are no admission of failure. Research shows demergers cost less, carry fewer risks, and eventually create greater value than disruptive takeovers. Conglomerate management is just ordinary company management, writ huge. Expansion, by judicious acquisition or organic growth, is a fine goal. But only executives who show over time they are adding to owners' wealth, not getting in the way, deserve market laurels. If that means more disposals and demergers and fewer self-destructive bids and self-aggrandising autobiographies, I'll be the first to applaud.[68]

Source: Hill, A. (2011) Breaking up is not a sign of failure, *Financial Times*, 24 January 2011.
© The Financial Times Limited 2011. All Rights Reserved.

Shaping your business is not just about personnel, of course. It is also about the culture that they embody. 'Tone from the top' is now enshrined in the UK governance code, which urges directors to 'ensure that good standards of behaviour permeate throughout all levels of the organisation'. But to maintain such a culture is hard work. One FTSE 100 chief executive I met pointed out that the message had to be reiterated constantly, via email, corporate blogs, and in person. Of course, there are other ways of ensuring the message sticks, too.

The death of Sun Myung Moon, founder of Korea's unification church, in 2012, provided a perfect excuse to write about culture – and cults.

You can take the cult out of culture

By Andrew Hill

Financial Times September 3, 2012

Among many proposals about how to restore a positive corporate culture at companies that have lost their way, no one has yet suggested a good singalong.

But around the world, the mills are alive with the sound of music. These days, my Tokyo colleagues report, Japanese corporate anthems tend to be hummable tunes rather than bold hymns to growth. But all new staff at Yamaha Motor still learn the company song, which dates from 1980, while a number called 'Romantic Railways' can be heard during lunchbreaks at JR Kyushu, a rail company. Big South Korean companies like to have a song and a motto laying out corporate values.[69] Employees at Broad Group, a Chinese air conditioner company now aiming to build the world's tallest skyscraper out of prefabricated blocks, chant their anthem ('I love our clients and help them grow their value') every day. According to the FT, Broad's micromanaging chairman, Zhang Yue, has also laid down 110 rules employees must commit to memory.

The use of songs to encourage a sense of community at work is not unique to Asia (studies have tracked down corporate choruses and cover versions from AT&T to IBM). But western sophisticates still tend to dismiss mass singsongs and prescriptive corporate codes as evidence of a 'cult-like' mentality. They say companies should, instead, encourage individuality and nonconformism, which can trigger innovative breakthroughs.

But here's an interesting paradox. A 'cult-like following' is exactly what the world's marketers hope to foster for their products, be they Jimmy Choo shoes, Krispy Kreme doughnuts or anything by Apple. Company leaders – Li Ka-shing or Warren Buffett, say – can inspire devotion and are often held in awe. Executives obsess about whether customers would 'evangelise' about the product or company and 'convert' their friends, even if they would shy away from comparisons with the late Reverend Sun Myung Moon's indubitably cult-like, Unification Church.

The loudest sneers at quasi-religious corporate behaviour usually come from competitors because cults are, by definition, very successful. A 'cult-like culture' was one of the fundamental attributes of companies that were 'built to last', according to Jim Collins and Jerry Porras, in their classic book of the same name.

➡

Some element of the cult is certainly useful to motivate staff and keep customers loyal. The line between a strong culture, cult-like practices and a fully-fledged cult is blurred. Rev Moon was expert at exploiting it. But how far along the spectrum between cacophony and chorus should companies go?

All companies have a culture, usually formed by what their leaders say and do, even if some outcomes are unintended. I was once part of an FT delegation shown round the *New York Times* newsroom by then editor Joe Lelyveld, who seemed to me to be the antithesis of a cult leader. He recalled how he had once idly nixed a photo of the back-view of a politician on the stump. Months later, he heard a group of sub-editors citing this decision as though it was a blanket veto from on high on the use of such pictures.

Leaders need to cultivate the culture, if only to prevent it growing in the wrong direction. How they do so will depend on the person – and the company. Not every organisation would benefit from Mr Zhang's 110 rules, though if I were a potential tenant for the 220th storey of his prefab skyscraper, I would welcome the attention to detail and devotion to duty of the entrepreneur and his staff. But plenty of chief executives distribute written principles and many of them post such values on the factory and office walls.

The critical difference between cultures and cults is that whereas a new leader can change a bad culture – albeit often with great difficulty – a cult's direction is impossible to alter. That is why textbooks suggest companies should aim only to be like a cult. When the charismatic, Ozymandian chief of a cult leaves, dies or goes astray, the organisation itself risks tumbling into oblivion: in the corporate world, think of the last days of Enron or Lehman Brothers.

So by all means encourage worship of your products. Draw up a weighty handbook of behaviour. Drill it into your staff with unison chanting of the company song, if you really must. But take care, and remember: a healthy culture is usually open to challenge from its followers; a cult never is. All together now.[70]

Source: Hill, A. (2012) You can take the cult out of culture, *Financial Times*, 3 September 2012.
© The Financial Times Limited 2012. All Rights Reserved.

Traditionally – as at the Japanese companies mentioned above – some corporate jobs were for life. But as younger generations seek to put together portfolio careers – or are forced by a trend towards 'mini-jobs' and zero-hours contracts to hop between employers – leaders will face a dilemma about how to maintain loyalty, and even continuity. Training may be the key.

Who will train the new generation of 'plug and play' workers?

By Andrew Hill

Financial Times January 26, 2015

Mary Barra is a lifer, born and bred to do the job she now holds. But as General Motors' chief executive pointed out in an interview last week at the World Economic Forum, few young Americans now anticipate spending their lives in the warm embrace of a single employer, as she has.

Ms Barra was not the only executive at Davos to point to surveys that suggest American 'millennials' now expect to do between 15 and 20 jobs in their lifetime.[71] It is a prediction that seems to transfix chief executives, many of whom have themselves risen through the ranks after long tenure at a single company, as they wonder how to engage younger staff. One way is 'to make sure they have career development and meaningful work', Ms Barra said.

I foresee tension, however, between large employers' offer of long-range, deeply thought-out, but often costly training and the short period of time most of those staff will stay put.

This contradiction could resolve itself in a number of ways. One would be that young workers turn out to be more loyal to single companies than they currently expect and that employers will be more loyal to them. But I doubt it. A truism that executives trot out more frequently than any other is that the only constant of modern business is rapid change. Ms Barra herself forecast that her industry would change more in the next five to 10 years than it has in the past 50.

Another possibility is that employers will fight ever more fiercely to acquire skilled workers from one another.

Opinions differ about whether this works. I heard one consultant last week extolling the way his company was now home to a bunch of tattooed millennials following a takeover. But another said companies put far too much weight on 'talent acquisition' and too little on developing future leaders in-house.

I agree with the second consultant. But many companies, particularly in the US, are impatient for 'plug and play' staff. As Alexis Ringwald, founder of LearnUp, which develops online training to get workers into entry-level jobs, said during a Davos session on how to develop a competitive and agile workforce, companies 'want the perfect person, made to order, ready for their position and ready to go'.

Even those chief executives who are trying to train workers internally have to be ready to induct staff rapidly into their companies. If the average assignment length for individual employees could be as short as three years, you cannot afford to waste too much time settling people in.

Vishal Sikka, chief executive of India's Infosys, told me last week that he saw his main role as providing the right 'context' for new staff. 'It comes down to how quickly you can absorb the ability of a person to contribute to the context you have created,' he said.

Unlike his predecessors, Mr Sikka was not one of the technology consulting group's founding entrepreneurs. He was appointed from SAP last year. He is also a fan of 'tours of duty' – mutually beneficial short-term agreements between employer and employee, a concept promoted by LinkedIn's founder Reid Hoffman. But as I have written before, the tour-of-duty approach leaves unanswered the question of how companies will in future sustain the strong sense of purpose and values that young employees find attractive, if most of the long-serving employees, who used to provide the backbone of big companies, no longer stay on.

Infosys and other multinationals continue, rightly, to set great store by their leadership institutes and training programmes. In the words of another chief executive at Davos, the way to bind staff to the business is to 'give them a sense of belonging'.

But as the form of companies changes to more collaborative networks it is increasingly hard to see what the workers of 2075 will 'belong' to. For instance, can a project, staffed by short-term contractors, connected virtually, and led by executives on two-year tours of duty, have a culture?

If so, who looks after it? And who trains the contract workers if companies decide that in-house initiatives are no longer cost-effective for staff who prefer to shift between employers?

Developing skilled employees for an 'on demand' age is an urgent priority. But as we slip towards a system that is based on mutual disloyalty, I fear it will become harder and harder to work out how.[72]

Source: Hill, A. (2015) Who will train the new generation of 'plug and play' workers? *Financial Times*, 26 January 2015.
© The Financial Times Limited 2015. All Rights Reserved.

Leadership lessons:

1. Never assume that each team member will be good at everything – an all-rounder may be stretched too far.

2. A team of *galácticos* will often be dysfunctional – better to shape a team of competent performers around a few stars.

3. The business model you adopt, or inherit, will have certain strengths, but it will never be proof against poor management.

4. Keep decluttering your business.

5. By all means shape a cult-like corporate culture for your company, but make sure it is open to challenge and change.

6. Never give up training: it is an investment in a strong future.

Growing

Growth is not right for every enterprise. In 2014, a Vietnamese app developer withdrew his Flappy Bird smartphone game because its success had 'ruined my simple life'. But generally success breeds size. Companies expand by acquisition, by inventing new products, or by entering new territories or markets. And with size comes stress for leaders who may have got used to the structure and style of the company that they founded.

Studies show we are getting better at mergers and acquisitions – practice, I suppose, does eventually make perfect – but deals are still risky, particularly if pursued for the wrong reasons. Expanding abroad brings culture clashes and new dilemmas about whether to export expat expertise, or import local knowledge.

Technology does help organisations grow. In Silicon Valley, entrepreneurs already talk about establishing 'mini-multinationals' from the outset, using the power of the internet and social networks to launch in many countries, with a multinational staff, some of whom may never meet face to face. Radical management thinkers believe this could lead to a complete reassessment of the idea of the company itself and what it is for. But I think the inertia of the established corporate world and, more positively, the usefulness of corporate organisation and hierarchy means that there is life in the old system yet.

New life in the idea of the big company

By Andrew Hill

Financial Times September 9, 2013

The life and career of Ronald Coase, who died last week aged 102, spanned the century in which modern management developed. That is appropriate, because Coase contributed immeasurably to our understanding of the potential and limits of the basic management unit that is the modern company.

➡

Even so, a few thinkers are taking a chisel to the solid foundations he laid. Author John Hagel has blogged that it is time to reassess Coase's view of the corporate world and come up with 'a new rationale . . . to drive institutional success'.[73]

In 'The Nature of the Firm', the 1937 paper that helped earn Coase his Nobel Memorial Prize in Economics, he sought to penetrate the corporate 'black box' and define why companies are needed.[74] In brief, it is because by co-ordinating activity internally, they avoid the high transaction costs that would apply if everybody did business directly with one another in the 'perfect' market beloved of 'blackboard economists'.

Since then, though, the technology-fuelled ability of individuals and small companies to collect and analyse big data and collaborate across eroding national and sectoral frontiers has cut the transaction costs Coase identified. At the same time, the increasing complexity of relationships within multinationals, and between companies and third parties, has, according to Mr Hagel and others, made it harder to manage the largest groups. Coase himself wrote: 'As a firm gets larger, there may be decreasing returns to the entrepreneur [manager] function, that is, the costs of organising additional transactions within the firm may rise.' Some utopians believe the biggest companies must now implode under the weight of management bureaucracy. A frictionless market will then be open for exploitation by smaller, more agile, more open groups.

But recent evidence – including Verizon Communications' purchase last week of Vodafone's stake in Verizon Wireless and Microsoft's acquisition of Nokia's mobile phone business – suggests companies are still bent on increasing their size.

For good reason. While managers may complain about the pace of change and their increasingly complex roles, they also take for granted the extraordinary online and mobile tools now available to help them achieve their tasks. Take the kind of analysis Coase himself carried out. When he went to the US in the 1930s to explore the complexities of its industrial companies, his data sources included the Chicago phone directory, whose variety of specialist providers of goods and services was a revelation. As recently as 1991, in his Nobel Prize acceptance lecture, he urged academics to dig into corporate contracts, laboriously drawn together in university databases.[75] These days, both analytical exercises can be carried out on a much larger scale. With similar tools, managers should be capable of overseeing and running larger and more complex enterprises.

Most companies have flattened their hierarchies, eliminating middle managers and improving efficiency. Many are exploring new ways to collaborate with the crowd beyond their formal corporate boundaries.

But as Ray Fisman and Tim Sullivan point out in their recent book *The Org*, a Coasean hymn to the necessity and durability of organisations, technology has also prompted some companies to bring more services in-house. They point out how Lowe's, the US home improvement chain, hired fewer freelance truckers (who drove more carefully than company-employed drivers) once onboard computers allowed managers to monitor and co-ordinate the fleet more easily.

Sometimes, too, it makes more sense to dismantle borders between companies to create a seamless larger entity. A Nokia engineer I talked to in Helsinki last week said the rationale for full integration with Microsoft became obvious when he realised it would allow joint phone development teams to 'focus on building the product, and not on the processes around the product'.

Trends in technology and globalisation will not necessarily tear down big, vertically integrated companies. They may well prompt managers to adjust more frequently the balance between what is best done within a company's walls and what is done outside. But this, too, Coase foresaw 76 years ago. 'Businessmen will be constantly experimenting,' he wrote, 'controlling more or less, and in this way, equilibrium will be maintained.' Long live that insight.[76]

Source: Hill, A. (2013) New life in the idea of the big company, *Financial Times*, 9 September 2013.
© The Financial Times Limited 2013. All Rights Reserved.

I stand by these conclusions even though I also believe that big companies need to adapt more quickly to technological change (see the Introduction of this book, and Chapter 9 on emerging new models of organisation), but I was rightly twitted by a reader for the examples I plucked from the headlines for this column. He commented online that 'Verizon is not getting bigger, but eliminating a major shareholder. Microsoft is buying Nokia because of desperation to expand from its declining core business'. That insight into Microsoft was proved dramatically right within two years as Satya Nadella, the software group's new chief executive, eliminated jobs at the old Nokia, wrote down the value of the assets his predecessor had bought, and scaled back Microsoft's ambitions in smartphones.

In spite of such lessons in the risks of M&A, deals remain the chosen weapon of expansion of many business leaders, including Mick Davis who, when I wrote the following column, was still the buccaneering chief executive of Xstrata, the mining company.

Chance encounters of the M&A kind

By Andrew Hill

Financial Times November 7, 2011

Whenever we put down a proposal to buy a company, the response has been 'This is an offer which is opportunistic'. . . Opportunism seems to be a dirty word (Mick Davis, Chief Executive, Xstrata, 2009).[77]

Colourful opportunists are characters from the M&A world's myth of combat. Here, acquisitions – and not only the hostile ones – follow weeks of hand-to-hand skirmishing, first between bullish chief executives and their more cautious boards, then between the company and its investors, and finally between the merging groups. This tale and its romantic corollary, the myth of true love – clashing armies, or blushing brides – are the stories on which the media thrive.

At the other extreme is the myth of rationality. Here, deals are justified with spreadsheets and statistics, and the tools of persuasion are net present values, synergies, discounted cash flows and 100-page slide presentations. When deals fail, many outsiders assume it is because larger-than-life CEOs and pliable boards over-reached, when the facts and figures were against them.

Nick Buckles of G4S is the latest to be slotted into this narrative, after the UK services group withdrew its £5.2bn agreed bid for ISS of Denmark in the face of shareholder opposition. It was a good deal, he said afterwards, but he and his team had sold it poorly to investors (they only had an hour to 'pre-market' it, according to a revealing employee briefing). Even so, much commentary has still focused on Mr Buckles' vaulting ambition.

In truth, most deals must balance machismo and maths. Get the balance wrong and your deal is doomed. It works both ways. Failure to grasp an opportunity can be damaging, too – and non-deals are invisible, so the cost of passing up such acquisitions goes unmeasured. What is needed is a way of reducing the influence of behavioural biases on these big decisions – a technique to intimidate the over-bold and embolden the over-timid.

Xstrata's Thras Moraitis and Hans Smit, a corporate finance professor at Erasmus University, have been working on a theory of 'serial acquisition options' that could make Mr Davis's idea of strategic opportunism less of a contradiction in terms.[78] Mr Moraitis has worked for years with Mr Davis, helping build Xstrata into one of the biggest mining companies through a series of acquisitions. Take out the self-justification, however, and Mr Moraitis and Prof Smit make an interesting case for more sophisticated financial analysis that would 'promote rational [takeover] decisions'. Their recipe is based on the value of each deal as a platform for the next, spiced with game theory and behavioural science.

Alas, as they acknowledge, you can't take people out of the decision-making mix. Bid success also relies on more than just choosing the right target and paying the right price. It requires careful management of what happens both before and after the deal is done. Some companies have natural advantages: unlike G4S's investors, Xstrata's major shareholder, Glencore, always seemed happy to put its money where Mr Davis's mouth was.

Two clear lessons: serial acquirers get better at doing deals – and it doesn't always help to prepare for years for a single big opportunity. In the same 2009 speech, Mr Davis warned that 'making strategic acquisitions is a recipe for disaster'. As Anthony Fry, who has seen deal action both as banker and non-executive, tells me: 'If you've long lusted after a merger, the risk is when it suddenly emerges, you lose your critical faculties.'

But even visionary and practised consolidators such as Sir Christopher Gent at Vodafone or Lord Browne at BP eventually went too far. With hindsight, the price Vodafone paid for its signature takeover of Mannesmann looks excessive. BP's integration of Amoco and Arco was flawed. The temptation for seasoned dealmakers to do the Big One – egged on by investors who have reaped the reward of previous deals – is often too great to resist.

Mr Buckles also used to have a strong reputation as a serial acquirer – of smaller companies. He has said he will revert to that more modest strategy following the ISS setback. While the corporate world waits for a tool to save CEOs from themselves – or, better still, a breakthrough cure for hubris – belated self-denial may be the best the rest of us can hope for.[79]

Source: Hill, A. (2011) Chance encounters of the M&A kind, *Financial Times*, 7 November 2011.
© The Financial Times Limited 2011. All Rights Reserved.

Mr Davis met his match within months when Glencore absorbed Xstrata, putting its chief executive and most of his team out of their jobs. There is likely to be a sequel, though: at the time of writing, Mr Davis and Mr Moraitis have returned with a new vehicle, X2, which again is aiming to put the theories of strategic opportunism into practice in the mining sector.

More timid leaders may prefer to consider partnerships, joint ventures and alliances. But even though the language is less bellicose than in red-blooded M&A, the same rules seem to apply.

Corporate marriages often end in divorce

By Andrew Hill

Financial Times July 25, 2011

Re-reading the first joyful tidings of business partnerships that have since gone bad is a little like looking at the wedding photographs of a couple on the verge of divorce.

Welcoming a 'comprehensive partnership' with Volkswagen in December 2009, Osamu Suzuki, the Japanese carmaker's chairman, said he was 'very much impressed about the enthusiasm of VW towards manufacture of splendid automobiles'. Earlier this month, as tensions between the two companies erupted, he blogged gloomily that VW 'might have come to think that they wanted to take control'.

Similarly, when Abilio Diniz, the Brazilian supermarket tycoon, deepened his partnership with Casino of France in 2005, he hailed the 'excellent relationship' with the French retailer. In June, however, it emerged he had proposed a deal with Casino's arch-rival, Carrefour. But in an interview, Mr Diniz made it sound as though he was the jilted party: 'Since this came out, [Casino boss Jean-Charles Naouri] hasn't called . . . still, I'm not bitter.'

At least the Casino-Diniz alliance, struck in 1999 and now at an uneasy standoff, has lasted longer than the rough average of four to seven years for such deals. The 1997 phone-making venture between Lucent and Philips ('This is a case where one and one equals three,' enthused the head of the joint company) collapsed within 16 months (Philips: 'We were sold a complete pup.')

Like marriages, business alliances involve people. People can be trusting, optimistic and tolerant, but also weak, overbearing and devious.

Keith Glaister, dean of the University of Sheffield's management school, says it is hard to know how many partnerships are struck annually, let alone how many endure. Unlike full bids, there is no official record. The long-standing assumption, though, is that between half and two-thirds fail.

Yet collaboration is all the rage. Serious businesspeople are again bandying about the word 'co-opetition' – whose ugliness reflects the potential awkwardness of the working truce between sworn enemies it describes. Companies had better get better at partnerships – or find ways of insuring themselves against their most common flaws.

A first step is to curb over-optimism. Launch press releases are so much PR flim-flam. But they often betray an underlying attitude of 'it will all work out in the end' – an airy approach that comes from the top. Root such optimism in real trust, as you would a non-business partnership. Prof Glaister cites a joint venture struck in the 1990s between Yoplait of France and the UK's Dairy Crest. Reciprocal invitations to the Wimbledon tennis tournament and the French countryside for the lead executives put the cream on top of that successful deal.

A second safeguard is to confront partners' natural unwillingness to consider break-up and its consequences. Here the matrimonial parallels should, but frequently do not, break down. The reluctance of lovers to discuss prenuptial agreements is understandable. But the attraction of a loose business alliance – versus the stark irreversibility of a full merger – should not distract from the need for some rules. Legal agreements must take account of a likely exit, any looming threats and the value the two sides expect to derive from the venture. Review these documents regularly. Too often, they gather dust until human relations change or sour. By then, it's too late.

Finally, pay attention to what everyone knows. Casino should have wondered in 2005 whether a restless and notoriously controlling partner like Mr Diniz would ever cede power. VW and Suzuki should have considered the wreckage of past automotive alliances and the potential incompatibility of the German company, under the ambitious Ferdinand Piëch, and the Japanese one under a protective patriarch such as Mr Suzuki.

Plenty of partnerships don't make the headlines. In a few sectors, notably pharmaceuticals, they are more common and largely successful. Such deals are carefully targeted by geography or product. The framework of mutual interest is well established. Larger-than-life personalities plighting their troth and looking towards a bright tomorrow rarely feature. It's not very romantic. But business partnerships would be more durable if the joys of the partnering part were offset more frequently by the realities of the business bit.[80]

FT

Source: Hill, A. (2011) Corporate marriages often end in divorce, *Financial Times*, 25 July 2011.
© The Financial Times Limited 2011. All Rights Reserved.

Whatever the chosen transaction, success will be determined not only by the choice of target, mode of financing, and determination of the parties to the deal, but also by the ability of both to rub along afterwards.

What Lenovo can teach us about making takeovers work

By Andrew Hill

Financial Times October 20, 2014

If you are wondering where your transformational merger is going wrong, you may want to look in the toilets. After Lenovo bought IBM's personal computer business in 2005, the Chinese company replaced traditional squat toilets in its Beijing headquarters with western-style sit-down bowls to put non-Chinese colleagues and customers at ease.

It was just one symbol of the attention to detail that eventually made a success of the sometimes tortured integration of the two companies. Others included switching to English as the enlarged group's corporate language from day one, to the distress of some Mandarin-speakers, and making sure coffee, as well as traditional loose-leaf tea, was available when westerners visited Chinese facilities.

Since January, Lenovo has announced the purchase of IBM's x86 server business for $2.3bn and the Motorola handset business from Google for $2.9bn. Just absorbing one of those large deals would be challenging, but Yolanda Conyers, Lenovo's chief diversity officer, told me the company has learnt from experience: 'It's gotten easier because we put the hard work in early.'

If only that were true of all companies. I chaired a discussion with 60 senior executives and advisers last week about how to turn visionary deals into reality. On a show of hands, virtually all of them had been involved in some capacity in an acquisition, which should mean that merger implementation is now a core skill for many. But while deal-making no longer suffers the 70 per cent failure rate of the bid-first, ask-questions-later takeovers of the 1990s, 54 per cent of a sample of more recent UK and US deals examined by London's Cass Business School destroyed value in the two years after acquisition.[81] Whatever language you translate it into, the message is clear: not good enough.

It is too simple to invite companies to stop dealmaking altogether. The problems encountered by Lenovo – and detailed in *The Lenovo Way*, a new book by Ms Conyers and colleague Gina Qiao – are enough to put anybody off the cross-border, transformational variety. Boards should beware of deals done for the chief executive's ego. But many large companies at least need to develop a technique for successfully absorbing smaller acquisitions.

A starting point would be to stop calling these deals 'bolt-ons', which is disparaging to the entrepreneurial businesses you are buying and implies that a bloke with a monkey-wrench can attach the new company in a morning. Merely bolting on an acquisition is to guarantee that over time it will rust away through neglect.

Cass research – and the experts I consulted last week – suggest that omitting to consult the company's 'people' people early enough makes it more likely a deal will fail. Involve HR even in the targeting of acquisitions and the chances of success should improve. Deciding who will be in charge is critical, but hard decisions on people and culture need to be taken throughout the organisation. The IBM PC deal was 'a struggle because we didn't know how to deal with diversity, leadership and culture', admits Lenovo's Ms Qiao.

Failure to integrate systems can also cripple a deal. Johanna Waterous – who, as a consultant, private equity adviser and non-executive director, has seen transactions from all angles – says poor information technology integration can infect an entire organisation with problems that last years. Her rule of thumb is that boards need to assume melding IT will take five times as long and cost five times as much as they first estimate.

It is a mixed blessing that consultancies are now always at hand with their Big Book of Deal Integration to assist the process. Advisers who have seen 40 or 50 deals to completion and beyond will know more about the practicalities than the nervous chief executive doing his or her first big transaction.

But it is the CEO who has to live with the consequences, and no manual can account for the myriad differences between companies and the multiple challenges that combining them will generate. In this respect only, Ms Conyers and Ms Qiao are ill-served by the title of their book (which was not their first choice). As they point out, an adaptable state of mind is more important than a fixed 'way' or template for integration. If you cannot be flexible, you may as well flush the whole rationale for the deal away.[82]

FT *Source:* Hill, A. (2014) What Lenovo can teach us about making takeovers work, *Financial Times*, 20 October 2014.
© The Financial Times Limited 2014. All Rights Reserved.

As the Lenovo deal illustrates, achieving some form of cultural accommodation is critical, even between two companies that are from the same corporate tradition. When Dixons Retail merged with Carphone Warehouse to form a single chain of electronics and phone stores in the UK in 2014, the leaders of the two companies chose a song by Kodaline, the Irish band, with the chorus 'love like this won't last for ever' as the soundtrack for a video about why they were doing the deal – a subtle acknowledgement that they were aware of the potential pitfalls.

It is tempting to assume that the cultural risks are lower when big companies absorb smaller ones but while bigger companies have a well-lubricated approach to integrating deals, moving too fast can kill the magic that was the reason for doing the deal in the first place.

How not to stifle your new subsidiary

By Andrew Hill

Financial Times April 15, 2013

One company may decide to buy another for its people, its clients, its products, its technology or a combination of all four. But how often does a company acquire another for its culture?

Bromides pumped out by companies during a takeover aim to reassure investors and staff that the two organisations will 'fit' well. But history frequently disproves those promises. Even if the bid is deemed a success, the benefits are often achieved through the larger company's total absorption of the smaller. Most of the time, the culture of the buyer prevails.

This sort of acquisition strategy leaves behind a trail of disgruntled, if newly enriched, founders. They will often be torn between devotion to their business and old colleagues and irritation about the big-company bureaucracy to which they must now conform. Frequently, they will quit as soon as they can.

Big companies have started to realise what they are losing by forcing new acquisitions into a blue-chip straitjacket. They are offering more independence to companies they acquire and providing some shelter from organisational overload.

In a speech last month, Dick Olver, chairman of BAE Systems, recalled how in the 1990s his former employer BP 'killed' the brand and culture of Duckhams, the venerable lubricants company it owned. By contrast, he said, BAE had tried to maintain the identity of Detica, a data management and cyber security group the defence and aerospace company bought in 2008. 'We have to recognise that these sorts of new businesses require a slightly different culture and perhaps lighter-weight policies and processes [than] big companies,' he said.

As I wrote last year, when the tension between Hewlett-Packard and its ill-judged 2011 acquisition Autonomy started to erupt, some integration – and, therefore, friction – is inevitable in any deal. Similarly, some parts of the culture of the new owner will be non-negotiable, however loosely the parent agrees to oversee its new subsidiary. BAE, for instance, cannot allow any business under its umbrella to flex the group's strict code of business ethics.

But best practice must run in both directions. The problem with a structure that guarantees creative thinkers autonomy and preserves their business in a discrete silo, safe from big-company bureaucratic nonsense, is that it could also prevent innovative business approaches from permeating to the rest of the group. How can both sides reduce this risk?

The new parent has to give entrepreneurial employees the chance to make their own mistakes, but entrepreneurs must also take the initiative themselves.

Tommy Ahlers sold Zyb, a social networking and data back-up company, to Vodafone in 2008. 'I did more PowerPoint than coding,' he says, describing the first months working for the UK telecoms group. He left after two years.

When Citrix, the technology company, bought his latest venture, an online work platform called Podio, he took a different approach, securing a seat at the table 'where the important decisions are being made', and a high-sounding title: Citrix vice-president of social collaboration. 'Even if entrepreneurs don't care [about titles], they need to look six months ahead and see how the dynamic of a big corporation will work,' he says.

At a Citrix conference in January in California attended by 1,000 salespeople, the 15 'Podios', as they style themselves, roamed about sticking fake tattoos to Citrix staff. Podio's sales techniques – it uses a 'freemium' model, making the software available for free at first – may not work for all the larger companies' products. But according to Mr Ahlers, the Podios' unconventional attempt to break the ice with their new colleagues may at least prompt Citrix executives to consider alternative approaches.

The approach of serial acquirers such as General Electric, a rapid and efficient integrator of the companies it buys, is sometimes contrasted with that of, say, Amazon, which has allowed Tony Hsieh, founder of Las Vegas-based Zappos, the shoe retailer it bought in 2009, to maintain its declared culture of 'fun and a little weirdness'.

The best path, however, lies somewhere between the two. Don't extinguish the entrepreneurial spark in new acquisitions or hold it at arm's length from the rest of the company: seek it out and use it to rekindle everyone's innovative flame.[83]

Source: Hill, A. (2013) How not to stifle your new subsidiary, *Financial Times*, 15 April 2013.
© The Financial Times Limited 2013. All Rights Reserved.

Growth also opens up new opportunities, as companies become too large for their domestic market, or the home market matures, but the list of failed attempts to take successful brands or business models abroad is long. When Best Buy, the US electronics chain, closed its China venture in 2011, after misreading local buying habits, Kal Patel, then its Asia president, conceded to me that 'When you're very, very successful, you can sometimes do things that feel like they go against rational logic. Very good people look at the numbers and then they say: "We could change the industry".' It is a warning that all leaders could have pinned up over their desks.

Wanted: marketers who know their place

By Andrew Hill

Financial Times January 23, 2012

KFC tempura chicken strips get progressively spicier the deeper you penetrate inland China. Iglo's frozen fish fingers used to have four different colours of breadcrumb, depending where you bought them in Europe.

Two contrasting attempts by multinational businesses to satisfy local sensitivities. Yet while the first was deemed a successful tactic, the second was considered a costly over-specification. Iglo's chief executive told me that when he selected one coating at random for the whole group, managers who had fought to keep their country's recipe didn't even notice the change.

It is possible that somewhere in Europe lives an Italian mama who still boycotts her local fish finger brand because it looks too Austrian, or that in China there is a KFC regular who couldn't care less what his tempura chicken tastes like. But this should matter to executives: knowing which local preferences apply may make the difference between success or failure when tackling a new market or launching a new product.

John Quelch and Katherine Jocz sum this up well at the end of their new book *All Business is Local*, where the KFC tale can be found: 'The forces of globalisation have not yet come close to rendering place irrelevant,' they write. In fact, they say, generations of marketers have made a significant error by assuming they should consider the 'Four Ps' of business school orthodoxy: product, price, promotion and place – in that order. The ambition of the book, which runs from a discussion of how to display your ketchup on the supermarket shelf to how customers' sense of identity affects their perception of your products, is broad. But many decisions taken by executives overseeing global groups must come back to the specific question of how far to standardise their goods for a global audience, or customise it for a local one.

Ikea, the Swedish retailer, is a natural part of the story of why 'place' matters in business – and not only because of its notorious policy of routing customers who just want to buy a lampshade past every other product in its range.

When the group started to promote its unfamiliar Scandinavian designs to customers outside Sweden, it took a conscious decision that it would 'shift the market's preference towards [its] own range and style', according to *The Ikea Edge*, by Anders Dahlvig, who was chief executive for 10 years until 2009. That was bold, but it evidently paid off. Last week, a cash-rich Ikea said it was forging ahead with a €3bn investment plan for this year, including tripling the pace of store openings in China.

But Mr Dahlvig believes Ikea may have reached the point at which it can no longer sustain its increasing complexity and size and still serve markets from Warrington to Wuhan. The group already has to tailor its range for different places – there is little demand for its big sofas in space-constrained Chinese cities, for example. The next step, Mr Dahlvig told me last week, should be to break it up into geographical units: 'They would be able to develop in different directions, they would see different innovations, and they would be closer to the needs of the customer in those regions.'

It is hard to imagine Ikea decentralising while it is still under the influence of founder Ingvar Kamprad. But a push towards more local autonomy would fit the international pattern identified by Prof Quelch and Ms Jocz. Country managers have enjoyed a resurgence recently. Multinationals have realised that the regional structures they put in place in the 1980s and 1990s, while adequate for mono-crumb trading blocs such as Europe, are unresponsive to diverse, spice-sensitive emerging markets. As dean of Shanghai-based business school Ceibs, Prof Quelch has first-hand experience of tailoring an international product – management education – to a local audience. To get that balance right, companies must now seek out managers to fill this demanding job description from *All Business is Local*: 'Home-grown marketers with local consumer knowledge, who at the same time are open to ideas from other countries.'

No easy matter. I used to think marketing was simple, compared with, say, product innovation. But – if their role is broadly defined, as it must be at global companies – practitioners of the discipline have a good claim to be doing one of the most complex, challenging and important jobs in modern business.[84]

Source: Hill, A. (2012) Wanted: marketers who know their place, *Financial Times*, 23 January 2012.
© The Financial Times Limited 2012. All Rights Reserved.

Last, there is growth by product expansion and there are few companies that have a more byzantine and, on the surface, bizarre set of product categories than the big Japanese brands. But there is an underlying logic to their strategies, as I discovered.

Yamaha's third attempt at cars will be worth the detour

By Andrew Hill

Financial Times March 23, 2015

'To become a bigger company, we need to try something new', Yamaha Motor's chief executive Hiroyuki Yanagi told the FT recently. The novelty in question is a two-seater 'city car', cleaner and more fuel-efficient than existing vehicles, that the motorcycle manufacturer could launch in 2019.

The suggestion seems to have upset analysts. They worry Yamaha Motor will neglect its core business, struggle to compete in a market crowded with tiny two-seater commuter cars, or fail to build a viable sales network.

But in a world where a six-year-old taxi-hailing service and a 17-year-old search engine company seem to be going into competition to develop driverless cars, it does not seem a great leap to imagine a motorbike specialist with six decades of experience transferring its skills from two- to four-wheelers. In fact, looking at the history of Yamaha Motor, puttering over to the adjacent neighbourhood is hardly an epic journey. If anything, its goal may be overly conservative.

Expansion is often a fight between sprawl and focus. When something goes wrong at large global companies – as, most recently, at HSBC – lack of control is often the culprit. More insidiously, big companies' inability to kill off unpromising projects can blight the whole group.

But fear of flying can also ground entrepreneurial ideas for growth. Executives' concerns about the brand being diluted or managers being distracted can stifle expansion into new areas, until an Uber or a Google comes along and does what the incumbents either did not think, or, worse, did not dare, to attempt.

Yamaha Motor's range has grown over time to embrace jet-skis, motor-boats, unmanned helicopters, wheelchairs and snow-clearers. Each line of business leads from another, with the group's engine expertise at the top of the family tree of products. Its swimming pool division looks like the odd one out, until you think of a pool as simply a boat with the water on the inside. Pools exploit Yamaha Motor's mastery of fibreglass-reinforced plastic, which itself grew out of its hull-making technology.

It is true that the group's earlier efforts to develop four-wheelers foundered on lack of demand, first in the 1960s, when it entered a sports car partnership with Toyota, then, 25 years later, when it designed then scrapped a supercar. But the biggest threat to its third-time-lucky tilt at the market is not the uncertain appetite of customers or the jam of tiny little cars already queueing to get in, but the fact the chief executive is in the driving seat.

Innovations often gain strength away from the oversight of senior managers, or even in direct contravention of their orders: Shuji Nakamura, who shared the 2014 Nobel Prize for physics, invented the high-brightness, blue light-emitting diode despite a direct order from his corporate bosses to stop working on the project.

A less extreme phenomenon affects new lines of business, according to Robert Burgelman, the Stanford strategy professor, who has studied large companies such as Intel and Hewlett-Packard.[85] He points out how many promising new businesses develop almost inadvertently within the corporate structure.

➡

HP's networking business, for instance, took off when a bored young engineering manager started 'digging around for something else to do'. It grew, then was disbanded, re-emerged as a profitable line, and was put on the block by Carly Fiorina (to avoid upsetting relations with Cisco, then a partner). Networking was finally reprieved by her successor as chief executive, who established it as an important part of the group.

Strategies for new business areas must combine bottom-up entrepreneurial spark and top-down recognition, allowing the business as a whole to evolve. 'The genius part is not having the CEO drive this process,' Prof Burgelman told me. 'The genius is in resolving some of this uncertainty, and having some evidence that [the new business] can actually work.'

The recent record of cars made by companies that were not already carmakers – including unlikely marques such as Kalashnikov, Messerschmitt and Sears – is patchy to say the least. But as engines get smaller, and car bodies lighter, the gap between Yamaha Motor's history in motorbikes and its possible future in cars must narrow. Provided Mr Yanagi maintains a light touch on the steering-wheel, his chance of reaching a new destination should improve.[86]

Source: Hill, A. (2015) Yamaha's third attempt at cars will be worth the detour, *Financial Times*, 23 March 2015.
© The Financial Times Limited 2015. All Rights Reserved.

Leadership lessons:

1. Growing organisations need structure.

2. Success in dealmaking is not just about picking the right target and paying the right price – you also need to get integration right.

3. Partnership is no easier – and sometimes harder – than a merger.

4. Involve your people people early in any deal – but do not forget to think about how to integrate systems, too.

5. When expanding internationally, do not assume your own range will work there because it works here.

6. Cultivate new product areas that are already bubbling up inside your company – but with a light touch.

Coping

The visionary parts of leadership and management – the hard-fought acquisition, the big product launch, even the signing of a big client – stir the blood.

But much of what counts for the day-to-day work of executives amounts to coping: coping with fractious staff, coping with difficult economic times, or coping with outright crises. What increasingly impresses me about leaders in business is that they manage at all.

All leaders are bound to struggle at times. Even among themselves, they must project an image of imperviousness to pressure that must in itself be hard to maintain. One unusually frank chief executive of a large UK company asked me once what I thought of a counterpart of his who had stepped down suddenly. He said he had been appointed at roughly the same time, but when, at an informal reception, he had confided that he had no clue how he was going to turn round the company he now headed, the other chief executive had responded: 'I know exactly what I'm going to do.' Such certainty, the first corporate leader said, was 'rather weird'. I agree.

I wrote about the gulf between the public image and private doubts of most senior executives in a column that appeared just ahead of the 2015 World Economic Forum in Davos. Gratifyingly, at the meeting itself, a number of contacts took me to one side to tell me that it reflected exactly their sense of anxiety.

Self-doubt in snow boots: the reality of Davos for most CEOs

By Andrew Hill

Financial Times January 19, 2015

Chief executives project an air of certainty but their real state of mind must be constant doubt.

➡

How do I know? First, very few of us go through a day without feeling bursts of anxiety about what we have done, are doing or will do. Second, it is the overriding message emerging from anonymous interviews with 152 chief executives for a study by Oxford's Saïd Business School and Heidrick & Struggles, the headhunter.[87] Third, accepting that many situations have no definitive solution – one of the characteristics of a paradox – could, paradoxically, be the surest way to handle them.

The CEO study, out on Wednesday, is cunningly timed for this week's World Economic Forum in Davos. The forum is thought of as the acme of corporate self-confidence. It is in fact designed to exacerbate executive angst. Every participant is afflicted by Stardust Memories Syndrome. In the opening scene of the Woody Allen film, the director sits in a train with a bunch of depressed or dubious-looking passengers. A clock ticks menacingly in the background. Allen glances across the tracks to see another carriage in which beautiful and important people are whooping it up. He pleads with the guard but cannot change trains. Davos in a nutshell.

Worrying about whether they are at the right party is, however, only a subset of the wider concern afflicting Davos Man and Woman. They are also bound to wonder why they are in the Alps at all, wearing snow boots and talking about mindfulness or machine learning, rather than inspiring staff, doing deals and tackling crises. Not all can reconcile the two conflicting demands. Rupert Murdoch called off his trip in 2011 in order to deal with the UK phone-hacking scandal. A coven of bankers pulled out in 2009 as high finance melted down. Mario Draghi, head of the European Central Bank, has chosen to stay away this year as he prepares for a quantitative easing announcement on Thursday.

Leaders of large organisations must balance the internal tensions of a matrix structure – region versus function, local versus global – and the demands of external constituents such as politicians, the public and pressure groups, which they often used to be able to ignore.

At the same time, their own existence is rife with contradiction. One CEO tells the Oxford researchers: 'You can't wait for 100 per cent certainty . . . but you can't just make a guess.' Another suggests: 'The areas I'm strong in are also potentially my weakness.' It is 'important to marry [my] gut feeling with the ability to be humble enough to ask', says a third.

Getting this balance right requires, another says, 'an almost insane combination of extreme confidence, bordering on arrogance, combined with complete humility'. Insane, indeed. The tension helps explain the short tenure of many chief executives (or, they might argue, helps justify the Alpine size of their compensation).

Inevitably, the temptation to take the easier path of command-and-control or micromanagement is strong. At the other extreme, a chief executive who disconnects entirely from operations risks turning into a 21st-century version of the discredited hero-leader. The boss who delegates day-to-day issues to his team so he can 'get a bird's-eye view, scanning the horizon for context without clutter', sounds as though he suffers from a God complex.

But proposals for handling dilemmas are unnervingly vague: the study advises executives to develop 'ripple intelligence' and 'harness their doubts', acts I put in the same category as herding cats or stapling jelly.

A drastic alternative would be to cut the complexity of the organisation itself. Jamie Dimon (a regular and outspoken Davos-goer) recently complained about the number of regulators pestering JPMorgan. Simplifying its structure would eliminate some of the intractable issues the chief executive has to confront.

Even if break-up is a step too far, multinationals still have to re-educate would-be CEOs. Taught to spot a paradox, some senior leaders at Glaxo-SmithKline realise 'I've been trying to solve this as a problem – now I understand why it never leaves my desk', says Kim Lafferty, the pharmaceutical group's vice-president for global leadership development.

In other words, for many of the most important issues chief executives now face, the traditional instruction 'Bring me solutions, not problems' seems to have lost its potency.[88]

Source: Hill, A. (2015) Self-doubt in snow boots: the reality of Davos for most CEOs, *Financial Times*, 19 January 2015.
© The Financial Times Limited 2015. All Rights Reserved.

I would not wish disaster on anyone, but crises – coming on top of the regular pressures that bear down on anyone in responsibility – have a tendency to bring out the best, or worst, in leaders.

We're sunk if bosses are first in the lifeboat

By Andrew Hill

Financial Times August 22, 2011

It was the product of a capitalist culture that put a premium on ever greater size and speed. It met all regulatory requirements (just). It was considered too big to fail. Parallels between the Titanic and the banks and companies that foundered in the financial and economic crisis are numerous.

Now an excellent book – Frances Wilson's *How To Survive the Titanic* – has refocused attention on J Bruce Ismay, chairman of the White Star Line that owned the ship. He survived after boarding one of the few lifeboats he had ordered for the vessel, earning opprobrium, disgrace and an unshakeable notoriety as the corporate villain in subsequent films and fiction. The story raises questions about how society treats modern business leaders who fail and what could be done to mitigate or prevent failures in the first place.

No one wants captains of industry to perish, but the sense that they should go down with the ship persists. Christopher Ward, author of another recent Titanic book, *And the Band Played On*, wrote in *The Spectator* magazine[89] that the audience at a Scottish literary festival cheered when he invited comparisons between Ismay and Sir Fred Goodwin, who piloted Royal Bank of Scotland towards disaster yet escaped with most of his pension. Lehman Brothers went down with Richard Fuld, but the estimated $480m he was paid while in charge continues to rankle. Having scuttled the *News of the World*, Rupert and James Murdoch of News Corp face heavy public criticism of their handling of the phone-hacking scandal.

Catastrophes have a tendency to reveal who really holds authority and who knows how to exercise it responsibly. Foreign executives who fled Japan in the aftermath of the recent earthquake and nuclear accident risked losing credibility, their jobs, or both, according to a new study by Egon Zehnder International. As one senior manager said: 'As leaders, we do not "choose" to stay or leave. It is our responsibility to be here to lead our organisations. That is what we signed up for . . . If I leave my team without evacuating the broader organisation, then I lose my credibility as a leader. If I abandon them, I resign.'

By contrast, without exactly exonerating Ismay, Wilson's book does make clear the confusion about his position and power. He was travelling on the Titanic neither as an ordinary passenger, nor really as an owner, having sold White Star to a US trust. The former Lehman and RBS bosses had more in common with the Titanic's 'pampered, celebrated and overconfident' captain (the big difference being that the captain did drown and his reputation was largely spared).

Ismay's great-grandson recently told the BBC, in consequence, that Ismay 'had no duty to die on that ship'. But even the evidence in Wilson's nuanced account suggests he had failed earlier in his duty of care towards the ship and its passengers. He certainly took the final decision on the number of lifeboats. 'The Titanic was already carrying 10 per cent more than the British Board of Trade official requirements,' writes Wilson, 'and anyway, why clutter the recreation deck unnecessarily when the ship was itself a lifeboat?' Before the credit crunch, bank board directors blithely asked themselves a similar rhetorical question: why encumber our bank with overcautious lending requirements when the system was itself deemed safe?

The desire to apportion blame and seek retribution after disaster strikes is human. It informed this year's UK parliamentary grilling of the Murdochs, and last year's US congressional inquisition of BP's Tony Hayward. Nearly a century earlier, it fuelled instant public inquiries into the loss of the Titanic.

Such hearings are unsatisfactory because they take place after the fact. Too often, captains of industry are brought on board with fanfare, then ditched with embarrassment. Shareholders (and, in family-controlled companies, directors) need to work harder to delimit business leaders' authority and clarify their duties before crisis hits.

Easy conditions of employment, overgenerous pensions and pay, insufficient emphasis on the risks (operational and ethical) rather than the rewards of the job – these are the corporate equivalent of the lifeboat Ismay stepped into. As long as these safeguards are provided in such abundance, the public will have to stomach seeing many business leaders simply float away from the wreckage they helped create.[90]

 Source: Hill, A. (2011) We're sunk if bosses are first in the lifeboat, *Financial Times*, 22 August 2011.
© The Financial Times Limited 2011. All Rights Reserved.

Coincidentally, I had reason to return to the Fukushima disaster and leadership in 2014, after reading an exploration by Harvard's Ranjay Gulati of what happened at the 'other' nuclear power plant, where damage was contained – thanks, it turns out, to some fine coping strategies by the leader on the ground.

Cool heads improvise in crisis and calm

By Andrew Hill

Financial Times July 14, 2014

When the lucrative business of advising on mergers and acquisitions was in the doldrums, consultants spread the idea that crisis management was 'the new M&A'. They wielded news stories such as BP's Gulf of Mexico oil spill, Rolls-Royce's disintegrating Qantas engine, and Toyota's jammed accelerator pedals to frighten clients into contracts aimed at helping them cope with such disasters.

As M&A activity has revived, so has its primacy as a money-spinner for advisers. But 'crisis' remains a bombshell in the boardroom. It is even modish to talk about business being in a constant state of crisis. The real art of leadership, though, is not being able to react to acute crises, which are rare, but to learn from such situations how to manage normal business uncertainty.

Plenty of companies have realised that fixed plans and strategies must be accompanied by a willingness to be agile, open and responsive to change. The language of the start-up is spreading to large groups. General Electric now teaches a test-and-learn programme for product development called FastWorks, conceived with Eric Ries, entrepreneur and author of *The Lean Startup*.

Yet for the most part, according to Ranjay Gulati, 'the way we teach leadership has a definitive tone to it', as though certain precepts will hold for all circumstances. To shake this orthodoxy, he teaches his students at Harvard Business School about Ernest Shackleton, the explorer who had to improvise to rescue his team when their ship was trapped and crushed by Antarctic ice 100 years ago. In the latest Harvard Business Review, Prof Gulati and co-authors have also examined the 'other' Fukushima nuclear power plant, Daini – sister to the notorious stricken Daiichi facility.[91]

Daini was saved from the after-effects of the 2011 earthquake and tsunami in part thanks to Naohiro Masuda, the site superintendent, who led a successful effort to shut down Daini's four reactors safely. Though he could probably not have rationalised it in this way at the time, Mr Masuda proved to be a skilful 'sensemaker'.

When humans cannot make sense of a situation that is beyond their experience, they become anxious and disorganised, even ditching basic principles that could help them escape the crisis.

'What holds organisation in place may be more tenuous than we realise,' wrote Karl Weick, an expert in organisational behaviour, in his 1993 analysis of the collapse of sensemaking during the 1949 Mann Gulch wildfire in Montana, where most of an expert team of firefighters died.[92] Though the circumstances were extreme, 'the recipe for disorganisation in Mann Gulch is not all that rare in everyday life. The recipe reads: thrust people into unfamiliar roles, leave some key roles unfilled, make the task more ambiguous, discredit the role system, and make all of these changes in a context in which small events can combine into something monstrous.'

The post-tsunami situation at Fukushima, where staff were panic-stricken and the way forward was unclear, had some of these ingredients. Mr Masuda's skill was not to deny the life-threatening danger, which was clear to all, but to foster a collective understanding of what needed to be done to survive it. By openly making sense of the crisis – scribbling his interpretation of the few data he had on a whiteboard in front of his terrified staff – he encouraged them to cope with inevitable changes of plan. Shackleton, similarly, had to adapt his ideas for leading his men out of peril on the floating ice when it became clear his first plan would not save them. These are the sorts of 'pivots' that start-ups – and, increasingly, large companies – must make when they discover one route of business development blocked.

Few leaders will confront the immediate aftermath of a tsunami; even fewer will be marooned on floating polar ice. But all are vulnerable to unexpected events that could force them to change course and trigger some of the responses Prof Weick identified at Mann Gulch.

As these vivid tales suggest, managing in a crisis is not just about planning. Leaders and their teams who become too wedded to one approach may be doomed. They must promote a reality in which their team can believe. But by discussing and testing other options along the way, they also have to keep enough uncertainty alive to enable their teams to pivot to a better plan before it is too late.[93]

Source: Hill, A. (2014) Cool heads improvise in crisis and calm, *Financial Times*, 14 July 2014.
© The Financial Times Limited 2014. All Rights Reserved.

The crises laid out in the two last columns underline that being able to answer questions of responsibility – Who takes it? How is it exercised? – are critical to successful leadership. If responsibility and, let us face it, blame are not clearly apportioned, it can make a crisis worse.

Such was the case at Barclays in 2012, when the bank was struggling with a series of scandals that had tarnished its reputation as one of the few big British banks to come through the financial crisis without having had to rely on direct government assistance. On the eve of publication of my column, Marcus Agius, then chairman, announced his resignation, leaving Bob Diamond, the American investment banker who had become a lightning rod for popular criticism of the bank, in place. But had the right person fallen on his sword?

The buck stops both at chairs and chiefs

By Andrew Hill

Financial Times July 2, 2012

Two elements of Marcus Agius's statement of resignation as Barclays chairman strike me as strange.

One is his reference to 'last week's events' having 'dealt a devastating blow to Barclays' reputation'. The way I read the regulatory reports on the bank's involvement in rigging interbank lending rates, the blows were dealt as early as 2005, were largely self-inflicted, and continued for years. The implication that outside 'events' have only now put the bank's image on the line is at best inappropriate, at worst misleading.

The other, more worrying assertion is that, when it comes to Barclays' reputation, 'the buck stops' with the chairman. I've met Mr Agius; the former UK chairman of Lazard is the epitome of urbane City of London suavity and this ugly Americanism sounds wrong coming from his lips. But it's not a question of tone: does the buck really stop only with him?

Technically, it seems to. Barclays has a very full corporate govern-ance code and a 'charter of expectations' for what those in senior roles should do. The chairman's responsibility to set out what is required for the group's 'culture, values and behaviours' is all there. Mr Agius also chaired the 'citizenship committee' with a brief to consider the potential impact of decisions that had an impact on the bank's image, 'including whether they will compromise Barclays' ethical policies or core business beliefs'.

So there is little doubt that Mr Agius was, in his words, 'the ultimate guardian of the bank's reputation'. He spoke on the topic regularly and publicly, notably in a 2010 speech on City ethics and values in which he suggested bank chiefs should use every opportunity to make clear that 'we are . . . motivated by, and subject to, a larger social and – yes – moral purpose which governs and limits how we behave'.

But he was not the only guardian. Corporate reputation is a precious resource. Everyone must look after it. The whole Barclays board, cer-tainly, had a formal duty to promote the right behaviour. In other words, this buck did not stop anywhere. It sat on the desk of every employee, from 'Trader C' and his fellow 'dudes' up to the directors. At all compa-nies it is the buck that should never be passed.

Beyond reputation, though, the question is how and when senior direc-tors should sacrifice themselves for the good of the company.

One advantage of separating the two main roles on British boards is that the company can maintain continuity if the chair or chief executive moves on. It is not the most important argument for such an arrangement but it has some value as a means of ensuring smooth handover. Even the cull of Royal Bank of Scotland's board – collectively responsible for the near-fatal decision to buy ABN Amro at the peak of the credit bubble – was staggered over more than a year, and Sir Tom McKillop, chairman, outlasted disgraced chief executive Fred Goodwin on the board, if only by a few months.

In the worst cases, however, the priority is not succession but cauterisation. Simply because some headlines now read 'Barclays boss resigns' does not mean the company has sealed the wound.

The logic of the chairman going first in a crisis doesn't stand up to scrutiny, in any case, unless he or she has caused the problem. If the root of the calamity is operational, the chief executive should walk. After the Deepwater Horizon disaster, Tony Hayward, responsible for day-to-day operation of BP, took the fall, while the chairman, Carl-Henric Svanberg, though heavily criticised, stayed.

Mr Diamond was not chief executive of the whole Barclays group at the time of the Libor fixing scandal (nor, incidentally, was Mr Agius chairman when it began) but he was in charge of Barclays Capital, where the trader-dudes worked. He had executive responsibility. If he was not the fount of corporate culture, he was a vital channel for it.

I'm no fan of the imperial US governance model but at those American companies where the chairman and chief executive are the same person there would be no question where the buck stopped. Mr Agius has decided to leave – with a parting wave to his 'excellent executive team' under Mr Diamond and predecessor John Varley. So be it. But Mr Diamond should not assume that the resignation of his chairman means he has dodged the bullet aimed at both of them.[94]

Source: Hill, A. (2012) The buck stops both at chairs and chiefs, *Financial Times*, 2 July 2012.
© The Financial Times Limited 2012. All Rights Reserved.

The following day, Mr Agius rescinded his resignation and Mr Diamond stepped down instead. Barclays has since gone through several combinations of chairman and chief executive, culminating in December 2015 with the appointment of Jes Staley, a former JPMorgan Chase executive, as the new Chief Executive, under Chairman John McFarlane. To me, it seems as though the bank is still struggling to assign responsibility for the next phase of its existence.

The commercial pressure on individual executives is great enough. But what happens when they face inevitable personal stress as well? Conventionally, this is not in the remit of boards of directors. But if a senior manager is struggling to cope, perhaps it should be.

Personal life is not off limits for the board

By Andrew Hill

Financial Times June 17, 2013

I once rashly asked the chief executive of a large listed enterprise if he was overpaid. 'I've taken no holiday and spent every weekend of the past 18 months trying to rescue this company, breaking up my marriage in the process,' he responded drily. 'So, no, I don't think I'm overpaid.'

For the avoidance of doubt, the executive was not Rupert Murdoch, who has filed for divorce from his third wife, Wendi Deng, and it was not Stephen Hester, outgoing chief executive of Royal Bank of Scotland, whose first marriage disintegrated in 2010. But each time I read about marital disharmony among the executive classes, I ask myself: is divorce the board's business?

In a technical sense, it obviously is. You don't have to have read Hilary Mantel's fictional accounts of Henry VIII's shifting matrimonial preferences to know marriage break-up can have profound political implications, particularly for dynasties of Tudor complexity such as the Murdochs'.

Divorce at family companies can complicate succession if heirs fall out of favour. Even when the investor base is broader, divorce can be destabilising if the boss has to split a large personal stake with an ex-spouse or sell shares to pay lawyers. Academics have explored whether a costly divorce dulls chief executives' risk appetite or undermines the effectiveness of their incentives, as they enjoy fewer of the rewards they get and try to hang on to the rest.[95]

In the case of high-profile figures such as Mr Murdoch, whose corporate existence cannot be disentangled from his personal life, reputations are also on the line. When details of Jack Welch's affair with a Harvard Business Review editor, later Mrs Welch III, emerged in 2001, they provoked prurient interest. The following year, in the messy prelude to a settlement with Mrs Welch II, the perks General Electric had granted to its former chief executive were revealed. Marital, public and investor relations collided. It was a turning point not only for Mr Welch's image as an unimpeachable corporate hero but in the story of executive compensation.

Yet even now, according to Didier Cossin of IMD business school, 'most directors' kneejerk reaction is to say [divorce] isn't a board issue'. Their squeamishness is understandable. It is hard enough to discuss such problems with a friend or family member. Even if the cause of break-up is a workplace relationship that embarrasses the company (the sort that triggered Harry Stonecipher's departure from Boeing in 2005 following an affair with a senior executive), directors can do little about the underlying problem without trespassing into a row about culpability that belongs, if anywhere, in the divorce courts.

Marriage breakdown says nothing about executives' moral fitness, but it must affect their mental and physical wellbeing. Divorce is draining, distracting and depressing. Wealthy businesspeople can throw money at the problem but few can insulate themselves from the emotional impact.

Most directors would accept the brutal trade made by my anonymous CEO-divorcee: save the company, sacrifice the marriage. But beyond fiduciary duty, they should cultivate awareness of the wider range of concerns influencing their senior managers' performance. The problem is that chief executives are often reluctant to admit weakness. Perhaps Mr Murdoch and Sir Rod Eddington, News Corp's lead director, unpicked the former's private life over a teary beer or two. For all I know, Sir Philip Hampton, RBS's chairman, offered his rocklike chief executive a shoulder to cry on in 2010 (though Mr Hester has said running the bank played no part in his divorce). But 'it requires a very emotionally astute chair to sense things are wrong and to tackle the issue proactively', as Simon Wong of Northwestern University School of Law and London School of Economics puts it.

Given what is at stake, directors who focus on the boardroom and ignore what's going on in the bedroom are making a big error. They may not be relationship counsellors but some are already rightly recognising the danger of executive burnout. Others regularly assess the psychological balance of the management and board team. One company secretary even tracks online references to her directors' private lives for early warnings of trouble. The fact is that overload can provoke divorce, and divorce can add to overload. Reducing the risk of both is part of the board's job.[96]

FT   *Source:* Hill, A. (2013) Personal life is not off limits for the board, *Financial Times*, 17 June 2013.
© The Financial Times Limited 2013. All Rights Reserved.

I predict that it will not be long before companies decide to devote as much time to the mental health of their leaders as they do to their physical well-being. For now, stress is a taboo. While new chief executives of companies such as Lloyds, the UK bank, and Akzo Nobel in the Netherlands have taken leaves of absence to cope with bouts of exhaustion, official explanations tend to avoid using the S-word. Being able to handle pressure is one of the basic requirements for leaders: to admit it has all got too much is tantamount to admitting the boss cannot do the job.

Simple and cheap ways of lightening the load – such as meditation – are starting to catch on. But in some quarters, they are still considered slightly kooky, as I discovered when I was invited to attend a mindfulness session at a big financial institution in the City of London.

Why must financiers meditate in secret?

By Andrew Hill

Financial Times April 28, 2014

I am sitting in a packed conference room, somewhere in the heart of London's financial centre, in an office I have sworn not to identify. It is quiet for a midweek lunchtime. In fact, it is silent. Along with the ex-chairman of a blue-chip company, a handful of executives and board members, a former senior central banker, a Buddhist software engineer, a Benedictine monk and 60 others, I am meditating. Or trying to.

The main thought I am attempting to ignore is this: if the benefits of such 'mindfulness' are as clear as science and millennia of human experience suggest, why is the financial services industry not boasting about the practice and rolling out the meditation mats across the sector?

Individuals including Lord Myners, currently working on reform of the governance of the UK's Co-operative Group, and Bill Gross, founder of Pimco, have talked publicly about how meditation helps them clear their minds and set priorities. A number of big US groups already host mindfulness sessions. They include General Mills, of Cheerios fame, and Google, whose people development expert Chade-Meng Tan is addressing this audience of financial folk about how mindfulness encourages compassionate leadership.

At the global financial group hosting last week's event, about 1,200 out of 10,000 staff tune in to regular updates about mindfulness, with 150 or so taking part in weekly meditation sessions. The participation rate has 'increased dramatically', says a senior executive. Yet high finance remains a bastion of corporate conservatism: fear of ridicule and industry scepticism means even enlightened institutions such as this one are coy about publicising such initiatives.

Half a century ago similar misunderstanding prevailed about the value of physical exercise for executives. I dug out an FT column from 1957 headlined 'Keeping Managers Healthy' [see page 114] that is full of delicious anachronisms (tip no. 5: 'Never travel over weekends except for pleasure and then never more than 100 miles'). The main concern at the time was that bosses refused to attend medical check-ups. Even then, the article cited a company doctor's view that executives 'generally have a better-than-average bill of health – or else they would not get to the top'. Only when CEOs kept keeling over from strokes and heart attacks did it dawn on them and their shareholders that the fitness 'fad' might mitigate the problem.

In finance a 1950s-era presumption survives that success is, to quote the same article, 'a tribute to [executives'] constitutions and physical and mental make-up'. Standing in the way of mindfulness is the worry it may be seen as quirky or 'New Age'. Yet brain-imaging research suggests meditation can alleviate anxiety and depression, which still plague Wall Street and City of London executives.

You do not have to believe mindfulness will lead to world peace to agree it is an obvious and relatively cheap way to reduce a growing business risk.

How, then, should companies go about introducing it? Not by compulsion. The biggest successes – including the nascent programme at our anonymous host – start at the grassroots and only later get endorsed by senior staff. Treating mindfulness as a productivity tool is unwise, too. 'This should not just be about making us better performers,' says the executive cited earlier.

Forcing God into corporate mindfulness programmes would also be counter-productive. Buddhist Chade-Meng Tan culls language that may be thought religious from his talks to Google engineers. But, as Laurence Freeman, the Benedictine monk, says, meditation is common to many religions. If it brought some sense of the spiritual to secular institutions that would be a bonus even bankers' critics could applaud.

Meditation must take a winding route to the workplace, much as physical fitness did. It should get there. Aspiring masters or mistresses of the financial universe would never neglect their physical wellbeing. Yet

➡

most gym regimes make disciples look far more ridiculous than a mindfulness workout would.

Even the FT's 1957-vintage tips for men managing multinationals advise some physical exercise ('gardening and fishing recommended'). Where meditation and mindfulness will prove their worth, however, is in helping modern executives implement tip no. 10 – still the most relevant and most elusive goal: 'Learn to relax.'[97]

Do's and don'ts for executives (FT, 1957)

1. Don't travel too often or too far.
2. Have at least one week's clear break in the middle of long tours.
3. Never fly both ways on a business journey.
4. If possible, come home part of the way by boat. If not, have three or four days at home before going to the office.
5. Never travel over weekends except for pleasure and then never more than 100 miles.
6. Keep your weekends completely to yourself.
7. Cultivate outside interests and hobbies.
8. Try and take some physical exercises – gardening and fishing recommended.
9. Have a medical check-up every two years until the age of 50, and then every year.
10. Learn to relax.

Source: Hill, A. (2014) Why must financiers meditate in secret? *Financial Times,* 28 April 2014.

© The Financial Times Limited 2014. All Rights Reserved.

Personally, I would welcome a little more evidence of self-doubt among senior executives and a little less self-delusion.

Self-delusion will sink Sepp Blatter just as it sank Dick Fuld

By Andrew Hill

Financial Times June 1, 2015

I blame Sebastian Junger. The success of *The Perfect Storm*, the journalist's 1997 book about a doomed fishing boat gave embattled corporate titans the perfect metaphor for what went wrong on their watch.

So here is Dick Fuld, former head of Lehman Brothers, in his first voluntary public appearance since its collapse, explaining last week why the bank went down in 2008: 'It isn't just one single thing, it's all these things taken together: I refer to it as a perfect storm.' And here is Sepp Blatter, Fifa president, as he prepared the way for his re-election at football's governing body in Switzerland. Last week's arrests of Fifa officials, he told delegates, 'unleashed a real storm'.

Blaming extreme weather is popular with controversial leaders, for good reason. The image of navigating through a tempest conveys personal authority and bravery but also lets them plead helpless innocence of the causes and consequences of what is happening. It is the false-heroic middle way between having to admit you are a fool, who had no idea what was going on, or a knave, who fostered the scandal. Instead, they can look like hard-bitten captains on the bridge, braced against the monstrous waves and wrestling with the wheel, while the elements conspire against them.

These are great days for collectors of leadership brass neck. In China, Li Hejun, chairman of Hanergy, the solar-panel maker, declared last week that talk of an investigation into the company was 'purely rumour, there is no such possibility' and said he would be 'the first to know if the authorities were really planning a probe'. Hours after Xinhua, China's official news agency, aired the interview, the Hong Kong watchdog confirmed it was investigating the affairs of Hanergy Thin Film Power, the group's listed entity, whose soaring share price crashed last month.

These are not necessarily lies. In Hanergy's case, the Hong Kong investigation may have been covert, and it is not clear exactly when Mr Li recorded his interview. As for Lehman, it is true that no 'one single thing' did for the bank. Mr Blatter's earlier protest that he 'cannot monitor everyone all of the time' is a statement of the obvious, familiar to anyone who has ever run a large organisation.

But there is something more corrosive than leaders lying to the outside world and that is leaders deceiving themselves.

Self-belief is a vital part of being an effective leader. Admitting to weakness is taboo. But it is easy for leaders to become overconfident and to start governing just by asserting the facts as they understand them and ignoring others' legitimate concerns: 'Hanergy has never been so good in our history' (Li); 'Let this be the turning point' (Blatter).

Mr Fuld has had nearly seven years since the financial crisis to ponder what really happened in 2008. But he is still trying to shape the narrative.

Plenty of chroniclers of the meltdown do believe, like Mr Fuld, that the US government was partly responsible for what occurred. Few would agree, however, that Lehman was a model of prudence, protected, as Mr Fuld put it last week, by '27,000 risk managers' in the form of its stockholding employees. On the contrary, as Bethany McLean and Joe Nocera wrote in *All the Devils Are Here*, instead of trying to limit exposure to the US housing market between 2006 and 2008, Lehman 'decided to double down . . . by financing and investing in big commercial real estate deals'.

Later, Hank Paulson, former US Treasury secretary, told the Lehman bankruptcy examiner that Mr Fuld was 'a person who heard only what he wanted to hear'. Such self-delusion also plagues Mr Blatter. It is the signature trait of overreaching leaders and a clear signal of potential disaster ahead.

Compare the Fifa president's attempt to brazen out the scandal with the way key players reacted in 2001 as Enron imploded. Three weeks after the energy company filed for bankruptcy, but before the extent of the saga of its corruption and self-dealing became clear, Jeff Skilling, former chief executive, talked to the Houston Chronicle.[98] Remember that Skilling, who was later jailed for his role in the affair, had cosigned Enron's last letter to shareholders, calling it 'the right company with the right model at the right time'.

'What brought Enron down?' the reporter asked him. 'A perfect storm,' he replied.[99]

Source: Hill, A. (2015) Self-delusion will sink Sepp Blatter just as it sank Dick Fuld, *Financial Times*, 1 June 2015.
© The Financial Times Limited 2015. All Rights Reserved.

This was another column that came gratifyingly true: by the end of the day on which it appeared, Mr Blatter had announced he would, eventually, resign.

Leadership lessons:

1. Learn to live with leadership's contradictions.

2. Ensure roles and responsibilities are clear, before disasters occur.

3. Planning can only go so far in a crisis, and may trap teams in the wrong approach, so. . .

4. . . . stay flexible and encourage your team to make sense of the situation themselves.

5. Beware the assumption that only one person is responsible when something goes wrong.

6. Keep an eye out for the personal problems that may be weighing on key team members.

7. Self-doubt is natural and manageable, but self-delusion is fatal.

Sharing

Autocracy has lorded it over democracy at big companies for most of the nearly two centuries that corporate organisations have existed.

The reason is, in part, that companies mostly start with one or two entrepreneurs, whose drive and imagination fuel growth. Even when entrepreneurial vigour is not sufficient to sustain the organisation, the system of professional management that replaces it replicates a natural hierarchical structure.

But this pyramid structure is no longer the only or even the obvious choice for new enterprises. As I pointed out in Chapter 5, alternative forms have always existed – partnerships, co-operatives, mutuals – and the financial crisis gave new impetus to them and to employee-owned models. Networks, powered by the internet, are now easier to establish and sustain. Even within large companies, the need to cultivate contact across divisions, sharing ideas, or simply creating the conditions for innovation, has never been greater.

Does this mean that hierarchy and structure will disintegrate? I do not think so. A few years ago, I spoke to Vineet Nayar, then chief executive of HCL Technologies, the Indian information technology company that became the poster-child for experimentation after introducing an 'employees first, customers second' approach that inverted the traditional pyramid, giving more power to the front-line staff. But he said it was misleading to assume that HCL had as a result 'thrown discipline out of the window': in fact, governance orthodoxy and the experimental model coexisted.

In parallel with these organisational changes, the way in which leaders think of the relationship between their company and society is changing, as even traditional corporate leaders recognise that profitability is not a zero-sum equation. Environmental and social exploitation may generate the short-term profits that some investors still require, but in the medium term they erode the social 'licence to operate' that all businesses require. Companies and their leaders share the same space as their customers and staff. It makes sense to ensure that they do not destroy it.

End of the imperial corporate leader

By Andrew Hill

Financial Times November 18, 2013

Not much unites Franz-Joseph I of Austria-Hungary and a flock of starlings. But when Don Tapscott, the business thinker, used film of murmurations of flocking starlings to conclude a presentation about managing complexity in Vienna last week, the mesmerising images unfolded alongside the forbidding presence of the old emperor, staring down from a gilt-framed portrait.

The coincidence underlined Prof Tapscott's point. Starlings, somehow organising themselves en masse to see off predators, are at the opposite end of the leadership spectrum from the all-powerful arch-bureaucrat, imposing his system on a highly complex empire.

The idea that organisations will simply shed their leaders and evolve organically to tackle complex problems is beguiling: it is a welcome challenge to the ossified bureaucracies that dominate corporate and political life and, as a gratifying side-effect, the question 'do you really need a CEO?' frightens the wits out of smug executives. But in fact, self-governing networks are about as likely to make leaders redundant as they are to restore the Habsburgs to power.

Old-fashioned leaders have the means and motivation to cling on to power, of course. But a better reason for the persistence of leaders is that they are still necessary, as even Prof Tapscott acknowledges. They are there to 'curate' the conditions from which solutions emerge, he says.

How, though? As Julian Birkinshaw of London Business School put it later at last week's Global Drucker Forum, inspired by the ideas of Vienna-born management writer Peter Drucker: 'We love the notion that as leaders we can create [the] conditions in which order happens . . . equivalent to the starlings flocking: it happens, but not as often as we would like it to.' By merely letting individuals organise themselves, companies risk ending up like Enron, whose talented staff were encouraged to 'run around the world looking for sexy businesses', in Prof Birkinshaw's words, while the original core values of the company went into meltdown.

Enlightened corporate leaders have many ways to perform their role without relinquishing the reins altogether. Rick Goings, who runs Tupperware Brands, oversees a sales force of 3m independent contractors.

He says he holds the network together with a shared sense of purpose – but at the same time, he decides which things truly matter for the group. Natarajan Chandrasekaran, chief executive of Tata Consultancy Services, taps the intellectual power of the many high-achieving engineers in his company by providing a social media platform that has, to his surprise, turned out to be largely self-regulating.

Leaders still need to choose the individuals to carry out the work, even if those individuals then decide who is best qualified to manage it. One discussion in Vienna last week, about the management of complex projects, yielded the insight that sometimes a project manager recognises that other members of the team are better equipped to head it. Either the nature of the task has changed or it has reached a stage that requires a different approach.

Finally, having set priorities, picked the right people, established a platform for communication and granted staff the resources and support to do the job, CEOs have to trust them to get on with it. Harvey Wheaton, studio director of Supermassive Games, a computer game developer, is a disciple of 'agile management', a highly flexible technique for project management that works on these principles. He says it is not easy for managers, who can feel threatened by employees' autonomy. Their first reaction is: 'You aren't doing what you were told. Go back to where you were on my spreadsheet.'

To cope, business leaders require an attitude that may be closer to that of public policy makers and civil servants, whose formal powers to dictate what should be done are often weaker. Michael Hallsworth, a senior policy adviser to the UK Cabinet Office's 'nudge' unit on behavioural insights, summarised the approach as setting goals, making sense of what is emerging, and steering and signalling, rather than directing. In other words, modern leaders need to stand as far apart from their Habsburg forebears as possible: they must be adaptable, open, and sometimes as anonymous as a starling in mid-murmuration. But as for the notion that they should abdicate their role altogether, that is strictly for the birds.[100]

Source: Hill, A. (2013) End of the imperial corporate leader, *Financial Times*, 18 November 2013.
© The Financial Times Limited 2013. All Rights Reserved.

I try to steer away from using the word 'stakeholders', but the fact it has become an indispensable part of CEO jargon is instructive, after years in which 'shareholder value' was the dominant mantra for leaders of publicly listed companies. Gradually, I think some leaders are realising that over that period the imperative to globalise meant that their companies' roots in society withered. In 2014, I was invited to the first Inclusive Capitalism conference in London – part of a rash of events triggered by the financial crisis to re-examine (or, it has to be said, reassert) the nature of capitalism. It was, by and large, quite a traditional set-up: mainly men in suits on stage, talking to an audience of mainly men in suits, in the gilded splendour of the Mansion House in the City of London. But perhaps because of the surroundings, one comment by a blue-chip boss stuck out.

Corporate citizens of the world owe fealty to us all

By Andrew Hill

Financial Times May 30, 2014

The head of a British multinational declared this week that he opposed the idea of companies that exist 'somewhere in the ether'. It may be 'odd to be British, but it's even odder to say you're nobody', this chief executive said. 'Who in the world would applaud you for saying that you are rootless?' The answer was, until recently: most business leaders and investors – the very people who were listening to him address a private session at the Inclusive Capitalism conference in London.

Global companies in the past 30 years have done all they can to shrug off the uncomfortable trappings of nationality, tax domicile and regulatory jurisdiction in pursuit of profit and efficiency.

Such a quest goes against nature. Sailors used to consider a sighting of The Flying Dutchman – a phantom ship condemned never to make port – a ghastly omen. But companies have made a virtue of their loose moorings and changeable identities.

They switch headquarters depending on the tax situation – as advertising group WPP did, from London to Dublin and back again. They wave the national flag to win local subsidies or support for new investment, then hide it when trying to sell their products. Sometimes they dangle the implicit threat to decamp if local regulation or legislation does not suit them, as HSBC did when the UK banking regime became uncomfortable, or use deals to arbitrage the advantages of different bases, as Fiat of Italy has done following its takeover of Chrysler. Meanwhile, brand managers play up specific national characteristics (French style, British quality, German engineering) in advertising; or deftly carry on business behind names that offer few clues as to national identity, such as Accenture, Infosys or Diageo.

To trade successfully in as many markets as possible, companies have become chameleons. In the process, they have twisted the original hippie slogan for sustainable living – 'think global, act local' – into that ugliest of management terms: 'glocal'.

This global orthodoxy has undoubtedly yielded benefits for companies, their investors and their customers. But, as the British chief executive's remarks suggest, public tolerance for such shape-shifting has its limits – and Pfizer's failed attempt to take over AstraZeneca has marked out the boundaries. The public and politicians saw through Pfizer's plan to form an even bigger global pharmaceutical group, based in large part on fiscal expediency. One unlovable, nominally American dealmaker wanted to buy a rival that *The Economist* calculated to be only about 12 per cent 'British', based on factors such as employees' nationalities and where it sells its wares.[101] The failed Pfizer-AstraZeneca deal also shows that, for a multinational company, trying to re-establish community ties means more than picking a flag. In fact, nationality – which whips up debate about protectionism and national champions – is an unhelpful way to measure the depth of a company's commitment to where it lives.

The chairman of another British company says he prefers to emphasise the national heritage of his group, which gives him the freedom to hunt for contracts and investments anywhere in the world. Binding his company too closely to the UK would, he pointed out, also give the impression to non-Brits that they would never reach the top of the corporate hierarchy. As recent research has shown, the upper echelons of the largest companies are still largely dominated by executives from companies' 'home' countries. Such lack of diversity could hinder original and innovative thinking.

Roger Martin of Toronto's Rotman School of Management sums up what companies have lost as they have gone global, recalling the tawdry way in which Boeing – long based in Seattle – in effect put the decision on where to locate its headquarters out to auction to the highest municipal bidder in the early 2000s. Professor Martin writes in his 2011 book, *Fixing the Game*, that the aircraft maker finally settled on Chicago, which had held out the biggest incentives.

In abandoning the communities they once served, he says, companies make it inevitable that their executives will join instead an international community of shareholder-value-driven managers and short-term investors – a league that prefers life at 35,000ft to operating at ground level.

Multinationals cannot easily be unravelled. Many vibrant companies start as 'micro-multinationals', raised as international businesses from birth, on a diet of the web and globalisation. Some big companies have started to recognise the risks. As Prof Martin puts it, the clever modern company 'has to fall in love with every jurisdiction in which it has a disproportionate amount of resources'. The likes of Unilever and Nestlé say they are committed to developing mutually beneficial relationships with the places where they source their raw materials, a strategy that represents an advance on old-style corporate social responsibility by linking the core business to long-term goals for society and the planet. Still, the temptation to up anchor and set sail again is hard to resist.

Companies such as IBM and Cemex, the Mexican cement and building materials company, now aim to become 'globally integrated enterprises', extensive networks that sprout offshoots in whichever country is best suited to a given activity. But if they use this model merely to relocate operations more frequently, based on considerations of tax, cost and efficiency, they will never build the local links that underpin long-term success.

Lawrence Summers, former US Treasury secretary, told the same Inclusive Capitalism conference that 'business has always felt a responsibility to its location because it's had a stake in the success of the place where it is headquartered and the place where its workers live.' The challenge is to replicate that bond in a world where national borders are permeable and businesses can burst out of the walls that once confined them.

International companies may never again be able or willing to settle on a single place they call home. But they need to find new ways to put down roots in all the places they touch – or risk losing not only their cultural bearings but the public trust on which they depend.[102]

 Source: Hill, A. (2014) Corporate citizens of the world owe fealty to us all, *Financial Times,* 30 May 2014.
© The Financial Times Limited 2014. All Rights Reserved.

It is a downside of writing about management that the same corporate examples recur in the books, articles and case studies that cross my desk: Johnson & Johnson's recall of potentially tainted Tylenol, as a model of crisis management; General Electric's portable electrocardiograph as an example of reverse innovation (an odd coinage – surely this is merely 'innovation' that did not originate in the US or Europe?); and virtually everything that

Apple has done, or is doing. One name that crops up repeatedly is Zappos, the Amazon-owned online shoe retailer that has developed a reputation for experimenting with new approaches to business. Zappos has excelled itself, however, with its experiment with Holacracy, which came to light in 2014.

Zappos and the collapse of corporate hierarchies

By Andrew Hill

Financial Times January 6, 2014

You come back from holiday to find your chief executive has given up power to a central constitution. Your team has been disbanded and your title scrapped. You are now all partners, each with an agreed role and a duty to support others whose work overlaps yours. Instead of allowing tension to fester internally, you will raise problems openly at regular meetings that promote positive action.

What sounds like an egalitarian dream is becoming reality at Zappos. The US online shoe retailer plans to switch to this manager-less system – branded 'Holacracy' – by the end of this year, making it the biggest company run along these lines. When the news broke last week, it generated valuable publicity for HolacracyOne, the consulting firm working with Zappos, which owns the trademark and sells licences linked to it. Business academics have already praised Zappos to the point of tiresomeness for its unorthodox style, so expect to hear more. But if the approach is more than a mere fad, what might more conventional companies learn from self-managing companies?

Quite a lot, I believe, but only if they discard some preconceptions and look to distil the most useful elements from such methods.

Self-organising does not, for example, mean ditching structure altogether, or getting bogged down in consensus decision-making. Holacracy – a cumbersome derivation from the Greek word for 'whole' – is based on rules and processes, points out HolacracyOne's Brian Robertson. He says adopting its generic constitution is more reliable than trying to copy cultures peculiar to the self-managing favourites of business thinkers, such as US companies WL Gore or Morning Star.

Even so, I think big companies run some large risks if they introduce self-government in one go.

One is that businesses built on the old model – including vendors, customers and investors – could be uncomfortable dealing with companies

➡

that have switched to an unfamiliar new structure. Zappos is owned outright by Amazon, which Jeff Bezos runs with old-fashioned micromanaging ruthlessness. He allows the shoe retailer a long leash, but what will happen when Holacracy clashes with Bezocracy?

Confusion is another risk. After PA Consulting abolished titles in the early 1990s, incoming chief executive Jon Moynihan had to quiz staff to work out who did what. He spent time reassembling the PA jigsaw when he could have been tackling its pressing financial problems.

Demolishing hierarchy could prompt talented staff aiming for a senior job to defect. Or it could force them to hide their ambitions, which merely pushes conflicts beneath the surface. Stanford Graduate School of Business professor Lindred Greer, who studies power shifts within teams, told me that 'even in Silicon Valley, [where] people pride themselves on not having hierarchy, many are hierarchically driven'.

Advocates of new models have answers to some of these objections – they rightly point out that titles are not always the best way to identify the most influential staff members and can add to confusion. A bigger challenge, as academic Morten Hansen commented when I wrote about new management models last year, is the lack of hard evidence that self-organised companies outperform their conventionally structured rivals.

Research does show, however, that some underlying principles of self-management can change the dynamics of teams for the better.

Prof Greer and fellow academics have found, for instance, that, far from reducing infighting at senior level, hierarchy exacerbates it. The key to maintaining good relations between senior colleagues is not necessarily to flatten out all differences in rank, but to foster mutual appreciation of individuals' skills in fulfilling their clearly defined jobs. Prof Greer has likened this approach to King Arthur's round table, where individual knights each had a specified role. High-level teams 'don't just need to share leadership, [they] need to share respect', she says.

Self-governing methods take these insights a step further. But for most companies to adopt such approaches takes time, a leap of faith and an act of unusual self-effacement by their leaders. Here, however, is a resolution corporate executives can make straight away: if you defer to each other's skills, learn how to manage conflict, and share decisions, you are less likely to descend into pointless power struggles.[103]

FT *Source:* Hill, A. (2014) Zappos and the collapse of corporate hierarchies, *Financial Times*, 6 January 2014.
© The Financial Times Limited 2014. All Rights Reserved.

Whether Holacracy will be a success or a failure will not be clear for a while. Reports in 2015 suggested that the experiment was upsetting staff and Tony Hsieh, Zappos' chief executive, decided to take a 'rip the Band-Aid' approach to the next phase of the transition, offering severance packages to individuals uncomfortable with Holacracy.[104]

It seems to me that Holacracy, partly through the efforts of its promoters at HolacracyOne (Brian Robertson produced a book about the concept in 2015), has received a disproportionate amount of attention. It is more likely, as I suggested in that 2014 column, that hybrid models will emerge that pick and choose some of the best elements of different management approaches. Etsy, the craft marketplace that came to market in 2015, is one example of a group attempting to marry its distinctive approach and culture with traditional market expectations.

Why I hope Etsy survives flotation with its soul intact

By Andrew Hill

Financial Times March 9, 2015

After Etsy revealed its plans to go public on March 4, discussion forums for sellers using the online craft marketplace ignited with a mixture of those two great stock market emotions: fear and greed.

'It means it will be all about the shareholders and not the shop owners. I liked having a shop on Etsy and how they really seem to care about us . . . I can see that going away now,' wrote Karen Cassidy in New Jersey, from whom you can buy a knitted 'fun ponytail squid hat'. But Marguerite Payne, a San Francisco-based maker of 'one-of-a-kind jewellery', chipped in: 'Wait till the IPO hype dies down and the stock price drops. That's the time to buy some shares. That's what I did with FB [Facebook]. It's worked out well.'

The eclectic nature of the mostly handmade merchandise sold through Etsy, and its folksy approach (staff eat off compostable plates then bike

➡

the waste out to a local farm for recycling), make the marketplace easy to mock. The risk it will abandon those principles and turn into a soulless, profit-hunting conglomerate makes it easy to attack its decision to go public. But Etsy deserves support as a test case of whether such a company can survive listing with its management style and principles intact.

Chad Dickerson, Etsy's chief executive, wrote a schmaltzy letter in its regulatory filing,[105] outlining the company's goal of creating a more sustainable and transparent 'Etsy Economy' that 'transcends price and convenience, [that] emphasises relationships over transactions and optimises for authorship and provenance'. He might as well have written a one-line instruction to potential investors to scroll down to the serious financial stuff.

But it would be careless merely to discard the 'Letter from Chad'. The Etsy Economy may sound utopian; the alternative is an everyone-for-themselves nightmare.

The main reason I hope Etsy flourishes is that, for a commission, it provides a marketing and administrative backbone and an online community for some of the flexible, but fragile, freelancers and part-timers who make up the growing post-automation workforce.

A characteristically gloomy Nouriel Roubini, the US economist, told the Future of Work conference in London last week that a world 'where everyone is going to become an entrepreneur and innovator is not going to happen'. Perhaps not. But everyone will need a bit of entrepreneur in their variegated career. Research from Oxford Martin School[106] suggests 'jobs involving the development of novel ideas and artefacts' – Etsy jobs – are among those at lower risk from automation.

Whatever you think of bespoke cufflinks and hand-stitched oven-gloves, some of Etsy's 1.4m vendors will go on to manufacture on a grander scale: a second reason the company itself needs to bulk up.

A third is that Etsy would be one of a handful of companies – Natura, the Brazilian cosmetics group is another – that are publicly traded 'B Corporations', certified as following high environmental and social standards. Etsy's reputation is at stake if its B Corp score declines, according to the filing. So, I would argue, is the reputation of a stock market that cannot cultivate more such companies.

A final reason to back Etsy's IPO is that the larger it grows, the louder it can shout. As economist Laura Tyson pointed out at last week's conference, it is unreasonable for techno-optimists to expect people to be resilient if their post-automation jobs 'do not provide a living standard consistent with the society in which they live'. Etsy, which has in the past struggled to convince policy makers to listen, can help make the case for government to support its growing community of free agents.

The dark parallel invoked on Etsy forums is eBay. It has turned itself from an auction site for enthusiastic amateurs into a more conventional ecommerce company. The fear is a profit-oriented Etsy may ditch its principles – probably along with the well-meaning Mr Dickerson – and force merchants to seek shelter elsewhere.

I hope not. Even if you have not (yet) had to adopt a sideline in repurposing old vinyl records as clocks featuring silhouettes of Star Wars figures, or stitching felt and fur together to make panther-paw potholders, you should be cheering Etsy's next move to expand. Because if there is no room in the Etsy Economy for organisations like Etsy, we really will be on our own.[107]

Source: Hill, A. (2015) Why I hope Etsy survives flotation with its soul intact, *Financial Times*, 9 March 2015.
© The Financial Times Limited 2015. All Rights Reserved.

Etsy is a for-profit business – something that some of its more idealistic members seem not to appreciate – but in tapping a network of enthusiastic craftspeople, it takes much of its energy from the same goodwill that sustains voluntary organisations.

The volunteer spirit that binds a team more than cash

By Andrew Hill

Financial Times January 12, 2015

If you have room left in your 2015 diary, then volunteer. If you feel overwhelmed by work – the main reason UK citizens claim they cannot devote time to a good cause – then volunteer.[108] It will teach you something you can use to improve as a manager and as an employee.

It sounds counter-intuitive. Some groups run by volunteers are, frankly, a mess. Everyone knows of an amateur sports team held back by disorganised amateur coaches; a choral society torn apart by discord over what to sing and who should sing it; or a local charity bogged down by endless debate about its terms of reference.

Poor stewardship hurts the people non-profit organisations help. It is also bound to depress their many supporters. In the US, Canada and

New Zealand, more than 40 per cent of people devote time to volunteering every month. Those are the highest ranking developed countries in the latest World Giving Index.[109] In the UK nearly one in three volunteer regularly, still an impressive commitment.

Improving how charities and voluntary groups are managed is therefore critical. Peter Drucker was, as often, ahead of his time in spotting why. He wrote in a 1990 handbook for the sector that non-profits, from Girl Scouts to Bible circles, 'know they need management so they can concentrate on their mission'.

Rick Wartzman, of the Drucker Institute, says the management writer realised 'non-profits are as important for their volunteers, in giving them a sense of purpose and citizenship, as for the people they serve'. As a result of such insights, most big charities are now run more like businesses, drawing on the advice of corporate donors and board members.

At the same time, companies themselves now know, and often crow about, how their staff contribute to the community. They are finding ways in which staff can reap benefits from involvement in corporate giving campaigns. Ever since I heard a junior banker complain that his boss had threatened his team that their bonuses would be in danger if they did not take part in a charity 'fun run', I have worried about the coercion implicit in such initiatives. But no matter, they are usually well-intentioned.

But as Justin Davis Smith of the UK's National Council for Voluntary Organisations wrote last year, charities 'hear very little about reciprocal learning – what we in the sector can teach businesses'.[110] My own experience helping a school, a university and a charity suggests managers could benefit just by trying to work out why unpaid helpers keep turning up.

Shared purpose is one answer. Purpose is already a perilously overused buzzword in modern business, but it is built into the way every voluntary organisation operates. Peter Tihanyi, a consultant who had a long career in the area, asked volunteers in the 1990s why they came and stayed. The reply: 'Because they enjoy the work, because they feel valued, and because they want to serve the [beneficiary] population.'

Of course, unlike volunteers, many people work because they have to, and have little choice about what they do. But managers should still strive to achieve Mr Tihanyi's treble: merely by trying, they would increase the chance of developing a happy team. Their staff would, in turn – as good volunteers do – almost certainly attract similarly dedicated new recruits.

Volunteers tend to melt away if they are fed up or bored; paid workers are contractually obliged not to play truant. But a business leader whose team is physically present but mentally elsewhere is in a worse position than a charity head who can fill a gap with other well-motivated volunteers.

As for the main difference between employees and volunteers – pay – many companies already rely on staff goodwill at critical moments. Monetary incentives, beyond the requirement to offer a fair salary, are of limited use in keeping staff keen. Bonuses may even reduce the quality of work done. Softer motivational tools are underused.

The NCVO's Mr Davis Smith called on companies to commission voluntary groups to teach them how to develop 'a psychological contract in place of the "cash nexus"' and nurture engagement.

It is a great idea. But as a manager, you could simply start by asking yourself this: what would you do to persuade your staff to come to work if you could no longer pay them? If you know the answer, why are you not already doing it? If you do not, then volunteer. You may well find out.[111]

Source: Hill, A. (2015) The volunteer spirit that binds a team more than cash, *Financial Times*, 12 January 2015.
© The Financial Times Limited 2015. All Rights Reserved.

In the same spirit, social enterprises have much to teach their conventional corporate big brothers.

A bit of selfishness is all to the social good

By Andrew Hill

Financial Times April 9, 2012

The caricature of global capitalism puts sandalled do-gooders and corporate suits at opposite ends of the spectrum. Historically, the corporate social responsibility department was walled off from the boardroom, except when the CSR manager came to ask which cause the chairman deigned to support this year, or the chief executive was coaxed out to a community awards ceremony for some awkward back-slapping with his favourite charity-workers.

This is changing, thank goodness, as relationships evolve between companies and enterprises structured along business lines that put social benefit above profit.

According to Pamela Hartigan, director of the Skoll Centre for Social Entrepreneurship, not one corporate representative attended the first Skoll World Forum, nine years ago. At the recent 2012 event, not only were there dozens of companies on the delegate list, many had executives up on the podium, explaining the advantages and challenges of working together with social enterprises.

Some mutual suspicion persists. The likes of PepsiCo, Unilever and Novartis were perhaps too polite to voice during the conference any qualms about working closely with not-for-profit organisations. But other delegates had no such compunction about describing the concerns that still run in the other direction. 'A lot of what Rio Tinto does to West Australia is criminal,' said lecturer Bronwyn Lewis, who works with the mining company on a child literacy campaign, 'but there's a few people in Rio Tinto who actually make a difference, and some of them are quite high up.'

These days many social enterprises are not just supping with the devil, they are shopping for the ingredients and cooking the meal together.

I agree with Ms Hartigan that this represents progress. Social entrepreneurs can benefit from alliances with big business – and vice versa. In fact, what I find bracing about ventures between established companies and social enterprises is that their partners are less starry-eyed than the parties to many ill-fated corporate alliances. As I have written before, the success and durability of corporate partnerships often stand in inverse proportion to the rosiness of their initial publicity: see, for example, Suzuki's unilateral termination of its partnership with Volkswagen, or BP's unconsummated alliance last year with Rosneft.

Behind the aura of social purpose, the word most frequently used by Skoll delegates to describe the nature of their relationship with big corporate partners was 'pragmatic'. It starts with the right choice of partner, according to Rupert Howes, chief executive of the Marine Stewardship Council. It has linked with McDonald's to promote sustainable sourcing of ingredients for the fast food chain's ubiquitous 'Filets-O-Fish'. Social enterprises have got to 'cut the herd' of potential corporate allies, he told the forum, 'and work with the leaders that will draw the others up'.

Gene Falk of mothers2mothers, which has partnered with Hewlett-Packard to digitise and analyse data from its HIV/AIDS education programme in Africa, was blunter still. Not-for-profit organisations have to 'think what the corporate partner needs out of this [alliance] and go into it with eyes open', he said.

Nobody should be surprised – or particularly worried – if alliances are founded on self-interest. Keith Kenny of McDonald's Europe sounded almost sheepish to admit that some of the motives for the company's MSC partnership were 'perhaps a little bit selfish'. By ensuring sustainability of sourcing from its fisheries, McDonald's also ensures the stability and longevity of the suppliers themselves. Well, good for them – and good for the MSC.

Frankly, if more companies acknowledged the selfish reasons for getting together with business partners, their alliances would probably last longer. Likewise, the virtues of a good social partnership – transparency, communication, trust, patience – are precisely the qualities any joint venture should have, whether its objective is drilling in the Arctic or mentoring HIV-positive mothers in Africa.

There is a need to educate more companies about how to work in a self-reinforcing partnership with social enterprises. But the lessons big businesses can learn about how to run their hard-nosed profitmaking alliances with other corporate partners are just as valuable.[112]

Source: Hill, A. (2012) A bit of selfishness is all to the social good, *Financial Times*, 9 April 2012.
© The Financial Times Limited 2012. All Rights Reserved.

In the background of much of my writing about what used to be called corporate social responsibility – CSR – was an article that appeared, coincidentally, just as I started my management column in 2011, about the emergence of 'CSV', or 'creating shared value'. I still wonder whether Michael Porter and Mark Kramer's idea is wholly new, and not just a marketing-led retread of existing ideas (predictably, when I put this to Prof Porter later in the same year, he disagreed: 'It's fundamentally different,' he said). But it does provide a different lens through which leaders can see what they do as not just self-interested, but in the wider community interest. As such, CSV seems to me to be another step in the right direction.

Society and the right kind of capitalism

By Andrew Hill

Financial Times February 21, 2011

After the Four Horsemen of the Corporate Apocalypse have bolted, society usually calls in the Four Hand-Wringers of the Messy Aftermath to shut the stable door: regulation, pay restraint, governance – and social responsibility.

That is what happened after the Enron and WorldCom scandals a decade ago. It is happening again in the wake of the financial crisis. But this time, what used to be known as social responsibility, sustainability or plain philanthropy comes in the apparently novel guise of 'shared value' or 'constructive capitalism'.

Shared value is a neologism promoted by Michael Porter and Mark Kramer. It got the full 'Big Idea' cover treatment – complete with the fluorescent orange headline 'How to fix capitalism' – in the first Harvard Business Review of this year.[113] Umair Haque noisily touts constructive capitalism online and in his book, *The New Capitalist Manifesto*.

For all their differences in prose style – the first sober, the second frenetic – these theses have a similar thrust. They even cite some of the same examples: Hindustan Unilever's Shakti initiative for distributing its products through a network of poor female entrepreneurs in Indian villages; mobile phone-based methods to encourage micro-businesses in Kenya or Bangladesh; Walmart's efforts to minimise costs imposed on local communities. These companies are generating profits, in Mr Haque's words, 'whose benefits accrue sustainably, authentically and meaningfully to people, communities, society, the natural world and future generations'. Prof Porter and Mr Kramer make the even more radical claim that profits with a long-range social purpose represent 'a higher form of capitalism'.

Heady stuff. But is this higher form really that different from the self-interested variety that Milton Friedman backed when he wrote that 'the social responsibility of business is to increase profits'?

Advocates believe shared value initiatives are knitting together social and commercial benefits more closely than traditional corporate social responsibility programmes can. So Nestlé's intensive support for local coffee regions in Latin America and Africa improves the reliability of supply to its Nespresso division and the income and environment of the farmers. Beneficiaries, distant from the recent 'failure' of western capitalism, will increasingly start to see companies as the motor for improvements in their standards of living. Confidence in local companies should then underpin more lasting, socially beneficial partnerships between the public and private sectors, reinforcing a virtuous circle.

What is more, big companies are not merely bolting these programmes on to their core businesses, according to Mr Kramer. They are changing their internal structure to accommodate cross-divisional shared-value initiatives and hiring people to run them who understand the social and the business challenges, not just one or the other. No wonder supporters of old-style CSR feel defensive.

But many of these initiatives are not that new – the Shakti project is older than Facebook – and the impetus behind them isn't either. Prof Porter and Mr Kramer urge companies to see their decisions 'through the shared-value lens'. But business leaders must still calculate if a new market or a new way of sourcing will improve efficiency, productivity and profitability, whether the new market consists of poor villagers rather than wealthy yuppies or the new supplier is round the corner rather than halfway around the world.

The pursuit of shared value – or what Mr Haque calls 'thick value' – plainly cannot eliminate the greed, excessive risk and bubbles that caused the Enron scandals and, later, the financial crisis. Constructive capitalists are still capitalists. Like all markets, these new ones will eventually become subject to diminishing returns. At that point most investors will choose the higher return available elsewhere, even if it yields the 'wrong kind of profit'.

In her 2009 book *SuperCorp*, which prefigured some of these more recent ideas, Rosabeth Moss Kanter warned of the pitfalls for companies that make 'social commitments that do not have an economic logic that sustains the enterprise by attracting resources'. More companies are learning to reap commercial benefits from strategies that have a wider social value. That's great. But the basic job of coaxing capitalism in the right direction is the same as it always has been: find ways to harness society's needs to companies' self-interest and hope the two stay together.[114]

Source: Hill, A. (2011) Society and the right kind of capitalism, *Financial Times*, 21 February 2011.
© The Financial Times Limited 2011. All Rights Reserved.

Leadership lessons:

1. Set the framework for ideas to evolve – but then trust your people to get on with it.

2. Put down and cultivate roots in the communities where you work.

3. Foster mutual appreciation of the skills in your team, rather than asserting hierarchy.

4. Stick to your principles – it will get harder, the bigger you grow.

5. Learn from social enterprises and voluntary organisations how to maintain and benefit from the goodwill of your staff.

6. Develop business that provides a mutual benefit to you and your customers and staff.

Leaving

I would not blame new chief executives if they did not devote much time to their departure on the day of their arrival in a new post. After all, when there are clients and staff to meet, strategies to frame and immediate fires to be fought, it would look negligent to spend hours working out what a dignified exit would look like, and who might fill your shoes.

But plenty of bosses do spend time framing an escape route: working out the exit terms of any new contract. It is the reason why so many corporate boards are later embarrassed when the managers they chose fail, and the lavish deals they struck in the first flush of courtship are exposed. Few leaders, however, plan properly for what happens next, and continue to get succession planning badly, sometimes catastrophically, wrong.

In the case of entrepreneurial founders of businesses, it is particularly hard to achieve a smooth departure. A few such founder-visionaries go on to occupy odd and unorthodox positions, such as 'executive deputy chairman' (the title held by Mike Ashley, mercurial founder of the Sports Direct discount retail chain), that allow them to exercise their magical powers without having to take responsibility as chief executive.

But I do not think boards have much excuse if they do not ensure that there are succession plans in place for their senior executives. Too often, temporary fixes are required, some of which make governance worse: for instance, Stuart Rose, an acclaimed chief executive of Marks and Spencer, the UK retailer, tainted his legacy when he took on the 'executive chairman' role in 2008, for lack of an obvious internal successor.

The question of how long a leader should hold on to his or her role is an open one, as the next column suggests, but it would be healthier if most leaders, particularly of listed companies, thought of themselves as temporary stewards of the businesses they run – and planned accordingly.

All I am saying is give CEOs a chance

By Andrew Hill

Financial Times May 23, 2011

Many executives joke about being carried from the office in a box; few earn that right. Malcolm McAlpine was still involved in the day-to-day running of the construction company Sir Robert McAlpine at his death last week, aged 93 – 75 years after he joined the business.

His is a family company, where blood is often thicker than governance. Generally, executives get far less time to prove their worth. On average, according to a study just out, chief executives who left the world's 2,500 largest public companies in 2010 had been in office for 6.6 years, having been appointed aged 52.[115] In 2000, when Booz & Co, the consultancy, carried out the first such annual survey, CEOs were two years younger when appointed but spent 8.1 years in the job. Even in the listed sector, however, there are exceptions. Warren Buffett, 80, springs to mind but GovernanceMetrics International identifies 15 other CEOs worldwide who are as old, or older, up to Walter Zable, 95-year-old founder-CEO (and director for six decades) of Cubic Corporation, the US defence and transport technology company.[116]

What is the ideal age and tenure for a chief executive? The boss of one large US industrial company, in office since 2005, told me that five-year stints are too short, while 10 years in the job seems too long. So, by scratching a seven-year itch to change the chief executive, boards are timing succession plans about right. But the latest study shows that 28 per cent of CEOs still left before four years were up, while more than a quarter had lasted more than eight years. In hard times, a long record – even a humdrum one – comforts boards. Per-Ola Karlsson, a Booz senior partner, says 'the risk of shifting someone who is performing at least averagely is too great'.

I worry that directors are too quick to axe relatively new chief executives and too slow to call time on long-servers. That costs investors money, in the form of absurd signing-on, retention and severance packages.

Faced with a decision on whether to move chief executives on or keep them, consider three factors.

First, try to match the boss's tenure to your sector and objectives. A company in dire need of turnround might require a fixer at the top for a short period, to be replaced by a leadership team with a longer-range view when recovery takes hold. But many CEOs believe it takes two or three years before their plans even start to take effect. Churning the top job at any organisation where projects are measured in decades makes little sense. Work done for The King's Fund,[117] a UK think-tank, found that 'high-performing healthcare systems [were] likely to have long-serving senior leaders', for example. The same might go for energy companies or utilities.

Second, closely monitor CEOs' attitudes, not their age. Corporate gerontocracies must remain an exception. But don't undervalue experience. Shares in nonagenarian Mr Zable's Cubic have outperformed both the S&P 500 index (and Mr Buffett's Berkshire Hathaway) over the past 10 years. Malcolm McAlpine's family building company is said to have benefited during the recent recession from his knowledge of what had happened to it during the 1930s Depression.

By the same token, even youthful business leaders can easily move from innovation, through self-justification to ossification.

'When you're trying to get something different and the CEO ends up regurgitating the same sorts of ideas, he's not adding anything new to the mix – unless that CEO is a special person, who actively seeks out good ideas,' the US CEO told me.

Third, and above all, stay flexible by cultivating potential replacements – if possible, from within the group. Insiders last longer in the top job and they generate better returns for shareholders than outside hires, according to Booz.

As a side-effect of such forward thinking, you may save much of the money ill-prepared boards spend on poorly targeted pay packages. Insider CEOs arrive with a built-in loyalty to the company, an understanding that their reign will be finite and a knowledge that the next CEO is already rising through the ranks. Those are stronger incentives to stay sharp than golden hellos, handcuffs or parachutes. Why, after all, should any company have to pay extra to keep an executive who should move on or to get rid of an executive who may have more to offer?[118]

Source: Hill, A. (2011) All I am saying is give CEOs a chance, *Financial Times*, 23 May 2011.
© The Financial Times Limited 2011. All Rights Reserved.

A common executive thought experiment is to wonder whether it is better to take over a poorly performing company from a failed executive, or to inherit a finely tuned machine from a corporate hero. The much-debated question came up again when Philip Clarke stepped down as chief executive of Tesco in 2014, having taken over from his much-applauded predecessor Sir Terry Leahy only in 2011.

A stepping stone links Tesco's Philip Clarke and Man Utd's Moyes

By Andrew Hill

Financial Times July 21, 2014

Shortly after Philip Clarke made his surprising – and, it turns out, prescient – admission at a conference in March that his days as Tesco chief executive were probably numbered, the boss of another blue-chip British company asked me, worriedly: 'Does it sometimes take two CEOs to turn a company round?'

The answer is yes – and the second chief executive may well be an outsider.

The fact Tesco has chosen Dave Lewis, a Unilever executive, to replace the embattled Mr Clarke, is the most striking part of the change at the top of Britain's largest retailer. Choosing a successor from outside the company is always a big and potentially disruptive step. But for a company that has, since its foundation in 1919, grown its own chief executives, and successfully reinvented itself several times, it is a revolution.

It is sensible to cast the net as wide as possible for potential successors, but it remains an exception actually to hire a chief executive from outside. Insiders made up almost three quarters of a global sample of 3,143 chief executives analysed in the CEO Scorecard published last year by academics Morten Hansen, Herminia Ibarra and Urs Peyer.[119] Of the 30 S&P 500 companies that changed chief executive in the first half of this year, only five went for an outsider, according to Spencer Stuart, the executive search company.[120]

Conventional wisdom suggests boards should pick an insider to run a company that is performing well, and that outsiders do better when brought in to turn round a company. In that respect, Mr Clarke looked the perfect choice to succeed Sir Terry Leahy, garlanded as a retail genius and godfather of the Clubcard loyalty programme in his more than 30 years at the company. Not only were the two men Tesco lifers, they were both from Liverpool and even lived in the same street near Tesco's Hertfordshire headquarters.

The counterpoint, according to succession orthodoxy, would be the botched handover at Manchester United. David Moyes was brought in from Everton in 2013 to take over as manager of the feted football club from Sir Alex Ferguson, only to be dismissed in March before the end of his first season in charge.

But the similarities between the challenges faced by Mr Clarke, the insider, and Mr Moyes, the outsider, were greater than the differences: both sat shivering in the chill shadow of their predecessors.

Mr Clarke inherited a number of challenges from Sir Terry, notably slowing UK sales and the need to unwind a high-profile but ill-judged expansion into the US.

But his biggest problem was the idea that there was a 'legacy' at all. Tesco used to have a reputation at management level for anticipating challenges to its business and, more important, picking people from the next generation of leaders who would attack the status quo. At one point in the early growth of Tesco, as recounted in the book *Strategic Transformation*, Jack Cohen, the group's founder, and an up-and-coming Tesco executive once grabbed the swords decorating the boardroom wall and 'clashed like duellists' during a meeting.

Successful long-lived companies have to maintain continuity but also promote challenge. Where inertia sets in, it may take one leader to start the turnround – breaking with tradition if necessary – and a second to pursue the new course.

As it happens, Unilever, from which Tesco has drawn Mr Clarke's successor, is a good example.

The Anglo-Dutch consumer products group was once a loose-knit federation of national companies, described by one chairman in 1963 as 'a fleet of ships . . . the ships many different sizes, doing all kinds of different things, all over the place'. Gradual reforms did not really bite until after Patrick Cescau – an insider – took over in 2004 as chief executive, rebuilding and simplifying the management structure and cutting costs. But it is only under an outsider, Paul Polman, in place since 2009, that Unilever has reaped the benefit. Mr Cescau was one of the Tesco non-executive directors who finally decided Mr Clarke's time was up, and that an outsider was needed.

Every chief executive wants to be successful. But stepping stone CEOs are sometimes necessary to help a company across the morass to firmer ground.

Alas for Mr Clarke, the fate of such managers is that they are more likely to be judged as failures than the people who precede and follow them.[121]

Source: Hill, A. (2014) A stepping stone links Tesco's Philip Clarke and Man Utd's Moyes, *Financial Times*, 21 July 2014.
© The Financial Times Limited 2014. All Rights Reserved.

Interestingly, while Tesco's continued problems – later in 2014, it had to reveal it had overstated its profits as it fought to maintain its share of the UK market – have not done much for Mr Clarke's reputation, it is Sir Terry's that has suffered more since 2011. The consensus now is that he overstayed his welcome at Tesco. As one fund manager said in 2015, 'for the first 10 years, Terry Leahy did a very good job at Tesco, but he got overconfident and wasn't sufficiently challenged'.

Long-range thinking on succession might have prepared the way for an earlier handover of power. General Electric, which set up a contest between potential inside successors to Jack Welch in 2001, used to be considered a model in this regard. But Tata of India offered a good example of how to do it in 2011.

Tata can take a long view on succession

By Andrew Hill

Financial Times November 28, 2011

The pun proved irresistible. 'Mystery Ends, Mistry Begins' ran the headline in India's *Economic Times* on the appointment last week of Cyrus Mistry to succeed Ratan Tata at the head of the eponymous tea-to-steel holding company. If the succession was a mystery, it looked to have a pretty feeble final twist.

When, in August 2010, Tata Sons said it would set up a special committee to nominate a replacement for the founder's great-grandson, it stirred up enormous speculation. Global consultancies that make money advising on governance shake-ups opined that a governance shake-up was overdue at India's 'promoter companies', which often exercise dynastic control over a network of businesses. Professional managers ventured that only professional managers could press home the advantage India's family-dominated businesses had over state-owned Chinese rivals.

Ratan Tata himself made clear his successor would not have to be a relative, a Parsee (the minority community from which all Tata heads have come), or even an Indian. Prominent expatriate executives such as PepsiCo's Indra Nooyi and Citigroup's Vikram Pandit were mentioned as possible replacements. Carlos Ghosn was cited as an outsider who had bridged a similar cultural gap to run Japan's Nissan.

After this excitement, Mr Mistry's appointment was deflating. A Parsee and a scion of Tata's largest individual shareholder, he joined Tata Sons' board in 2006. He was trusted sufficiently that he sat – Dick Cheney-style – on the selection committee, until the other members turned their searchlights inward. He is not a Tata – but his sister is married to Ratan's half-brother. Virtually the only radical elements are his Irish citizenship (his reclusive father is married to an Irishwoman) and his age: at 43, he could hold the chairmanship from December 2012 – the official handover date – for three decades.

So, hardly a revolution. But on reflection, I don't think that is what 140-year-old Tata Sons, or even India, really needed.

Tata is big, complex and international. At a stroke last week, Mr Mistry became the most important Indian that most of its non-Indian employees (from Tetley Tea to the old Corus steel plants) had never heard of. He will face management challenges, no doubt. But leadership experts counsel against the appointment of outsiders, unless the company they join is underperforming. Thanks to Ratan Tata's untangling of internal fiefs over the past 20 years, the Tata empire is doing well.

The structure is still idiosyncratic. Tata's chairman exercises moral suasion, mainly through minority stakes, over 100 Tata companies, run by professional managers and independent boards. As Ajay Bhalla of Cass Business School puts it, he has to be a good steward, rather than a hands-on manager, 'and stewardship is implemented through connection with various stakeholders'. One elder statesman of Indian business told me last week: 'Cyrus is a good choice, since he is youngish, will have a long innings, is a known quantity, is highly respected and is admired by Tata Sons' directors.' In other words, he has enough inside knowledge to build on the group's legacy.

Don't underestimate the importance of that long view. When Tata bought Jaguar Land Rover in 2008, pundits claimed it had overpaid for the high-end carmaker. But if you work on a 30-year timescale, your assumption of what constitutes good value changes. According to Lord Bhattacharyya, a member of the Tata succession panel, Mr Mistry will help Tata 'evolve in a manner that's not destructive. It's easy to get some short-term gains and kudos, but he has to maintain the long-term aspects and culture of the company.'

His appointment will not send the hoped-for jolt through Indian corporate governance. The succession process has ended roughly where it started: in Bombay House, Tata's Mumbai headquarters. Some stick-in-the-muds at the apex of corporate India could take the outcome as an invitation not to look far when choosing their successors.

But before slating it as retrograde, compare the successful evolution of Tata with near-disasters at western companies, wrecked by overpaid professional managers fixated on short-term value. The real mystery is that so few non-Indian companies have sought to borrow from the virtues of Tata's long-termist model, not the other way round.[122]

Source: Hill, A. (2011) Tata can take a long view on succession, *Financial Times*, 28 November 2011.
© The Financial Times Limited 2011. All Rights Reserved.

In theory, family companies have an edge over their non-family counterparts in being able to look ahead generations. But blood ties can bind them to the wrong potential successors.

A patriarch Murdoch should have emulated

By Andrew Hill

Financial Times March 31, 2014

Leonardo Del Vecchio and Rupert Murdoch have plenty in common. The chairman of Luxottica, the eyewear group, and the chairman of News Corp and 21st Century Fox were born in the 1930s. Both are billionaire patriarchs of family businesses they largely built themselves but now share with outside investors. Both have six children from different relationships, and both have wrestled with the question of succession.

They differ in one crucial respect. As early as 1995, when I shared a helicopter with Mr Del Vecchio from Milan to Luxottica's headquarters in the Dolomites, he was already adamant he would not hand management to a family member. Ownership of the company would pass to the next generation, but trained professionals would run it.

Some claimed Mr Murdoch's decision last week to leave his sons the keys to the board, the executive suite and the strongbox that contains his share certificates also brought clarity. So it does.

By anointing Lachlan, his elder son, as co-chairman of News Corp and 21st Century Fox, and naming James, the younger, as co-chief operating officer of 21st Century Fox, it is clear the mogul has made the wrong choice.

Maintaining both ownership and management of a large family business more often than not leads downhill into further confusion, uncertainty and internecine conflict.

Some business dynasties can and do thrive across the generations – think of the Rothschilds or the Wallenbergs in Europe. Many founders of smaller family companies – among Germany's Mittelstand, for instance – are able to pass the baton smoothly to their children.

Businesses are also more likely to survive a handover from the first generation than from the second or beyond as the family tree branches out. But research on dynastic succession warns of the risk of 'heir underperformance', particularly where senior executives are drawn from the family.[123]

The late Tony Benn, the British politician who renounced his hereditary title, summed up one obvious peril when he said it would terrify him 'if I went to the dentist and as he began drilling my teeth he said, "I'm not a dentist myself, but my father was a very good [one]"'.[124] But irrespective of an heir's competence, Lloyd Shefsky, co-director of the Kellogg School of Management's Center for Family Enterprises, says the danger increases as family empires grow. Sometimes they become so complex that 'not only could [the son] not run the business, his father probably couldn't run it any more either'.

At the time of my helicopter trip, Mr Del Vecchio's approach was unusual in Italy – and for many family companies, it still is. Some Italian patriarchs still insist on total control. This can spark familial conflict on a grand-operatic scale. Bernardo Caprotti, who opened Italy's first supermarket in the 1950s with Nelson Rockefeller, handed over the majority of his Esselunga chain to his children, then retook control amid lawsuits and intergenerational strife. He ran the company until he stepped down last year, aged 88. But Mr Del Vecchio has held the line. His oldest son Claudio is a chief executive – but of Brooks Brothers, not Luxottica, which is run by Andrea Guerra under the board oversight of the family.

Andrea Colli of Milan's Bocconi University says larger Italian companies' realisation they need a more professional approach as they go global has coincided with the rise of a cohort of highly competent managers. Mr Guerra, for instance, used to run Merloni, the white goods company (now called Indesit) that is also under family control. In such companies, the family provides stability, but non-family management supplies the strategic and operational expertise that underpins expansion and innovation, through ventures such as Luxottica's deal last week to develop Google Glass eyewear.

Italy is only a forerunner of what is now happening in developing markets, where entrepreneurs are planning more orderly handovers, using western-style family offices to advise them on succession management. There, the founders of bigger companies are starting to understand that drawing a line between family ownership and professional management is 'do-able and may be their best bet', according to Prof Shefsky. In fact, the most depressing aspect of last week's Murdoch move is the signal it sends from the old corporate world to the new that it is fine to keep everything in the family, whatever the unhappy consequences.[125]

Source: Hill, A. (2014) A patriarch Murdoch should have emulated, *Financial Times*, 31 March 2014.
© The Financial Times Limited 2014. All Rights Reserved.

Unfortunately, this column backfired on me spectacularly less than six months later when Leonardo Del Vecchio, then 79, grabbed back the executive reins after Andrea Guerra stepped down, ushering in weeks of management turmoil at the top of Luxottica. In my view, he compounded his error by appointing beneath him not one, but two chief executives – an approach that usually means that the board (or, in this case, the founder) cannot make up his mind.

More than two reasons against dual heads

By Andrew Hill

Financial Times January 30, 2012

I'll say one thing for co-chief executives: two scapegoats are better than one. Since Research In Motion's fortunes took a sharp turn for the worse last year, its dual-leadership structure has taken a beating. With the BlackBerry-maker's decision last week to revert to one chief executive, the double-edged knives really came out for Jim Balsillie and Mike Lazaridis.

Four years ago, Canada's favourite corporate twins won a place on Barron's list of the world's best CEOs ('two under-appreciated Northern lights'); now critics are blaming the double-headed organigram for prolonging RIM's strategic agony.

These attacks place form above substance. The substantial case against RIM is that it has buckled under competitive pressure from an assault on its core smartphone market by two of the world's largest and most aggressive technology companies – Apple and Google. The worst that can be said about the co-chiefs is that they failed to respond quickly enough to that challenge. But that is a charge that could be laid against companies that had the supposed advantages of single-CEO, buck-stops-here leadership, from Nokia to Motorola.

That said, I nurse an innate suspicion of co-chief executives. Something about the just-married matiness of joint bosses rings false. Bill McDermott and Jim Hagemann Snabe seem to be reviving SAP, under chairman Hasso Plattner, but who did not cringe on reading Mr McDermott's assertion in a joint interview last year that 'we have a unique way of making one plus one equal three'? Wipro's 2008 decision to give the top executive job to two people was later defended by Azim Premji, the Indian group's chairman and majority owner, using similar mystic maths: 'We required the power of two, irrespective of the weaknesses of the power of two.'

Most classic justifications for co-leadership fall apart under scrutiny:

- It helps retain top management. But it is the antithesis of decisive executive recruitment to give both candidates the job, potentially confusing lines of authority to keep egos temporarily in check.

- It aids succession. This is the reason used by family-owned groups trying to give the next generation an equal shot at the top. Think point 1), but with an added dose of toxic sibling rivalry. The case study here is Robert Mondavi, the Californian wine dynasty. He appointed his two sons as co-CEOs in 1990, but it took the intervention of family therapists to help unscramble the arrangement after it went badly wrong.

- We can't split the founders. Co-founders often have complementary talents. But they don't have to be co-bosses. Over decades, Bill Hewlett and Dave Packard switched between president, chief executive or chairman of the computer group they founded. They never held the same title simultaneously. When founders outstay their welcome, the co-CEO arrangement can make it harder for a board to unseat them.

- Shared leadership is strong leadership. This may be the strongest justification. All corporate leadership is shared to some degree. Bob Frisch, a consultant, argues in his new book *Who's in the Room?*

➡

that it would be healthier for companies to recognise that most corporate decisions are inspired by a close-knit group of individuals – say, a triumvirate of CEO, chief financial officer and human resources director – outside the formal organisation chart. But the chief executive is solely accountable for the decision itself. 'There always needs to be a tiebreaking authority,' he says.

It may be significant that the current success of SAP's co-leaders comes under the watchful eye of Mr Plattner. Or that Mr Premji and Mr Mondavi were there to disentangle the arrangement. In RIM's case, where the co-CEOs were also co-chairmen, a falling-out between the duo could have led to 'mutually assured destruction', in the words of Lucy Marcus, professor of leadership and governance at Madrid's IE Business School.

For all the wrong reasons, boards will continue to endorse co-chief executives. Deutsche Bank's Josef Ackermann will shortly hand over power to two successors. The theory is that Anshu Jain will pursue the global strategy while co-chief Jürgen Fitschen will be the face of the bank in its home market. But to my mind, the messy process and outcome bode ill. Inevitably, all three men were at Davos last week – hardly a sign they're comfortable delegating or dividing their duties.[126]

Source: Hill, A. (2012) More than two reasons against dual heads, *Financial Times*, 30 January 2012.
© The Financial Times Limited 2012. All Rights Reserved.

My predictive powers were a little sharper in this case: in 2015, Deutsche Bank announced both Mr Jain and Mr Fitschen would depart, in what the *Financial Times* described as 'the deepest crisis of confidence in a generation', to be replaced by a single chief executive.

BlackBerry's travails illuminated another problem with succession planning: when and how to decide to move founders on. I think some technology companies, such as Alibaba of China, are sowing the seeds of future disaster by enshrining founders' rights in dual classes of shares when they come to market. That will make it even harder for other shareholders to remove leaders who have done enough. But that is a different discussion. The cautionary tale of Twitter helps describe the more general dilemma.

The mixed blessing of a founder's devotion

By Andrew Hill

Financial Times July 4, 2011

In June 2004, Mark Zuckerberg turned down an offer of $10m for his four-month-old social network. Four years later, Twitter's founders – Biz Stone, Ev Williams and Jack Dorsey – declined an all-stock offer worth $500m from Mr Zuckerberg.

Yet while the notoriously driven Mr Zuckerberg still runs Facebook, two of Twitter's three founders – Mr Williams and Mr Stone – have stepped back from their creation. Mr Stone said last week he would devote himself to developing new projects 'that help people work together to improve the world'. He probably foresees a place in history as a 'serial entrepreneur' – too often a grand title for an inveterate dabbler.

But his move raises the question of whether entrepreneurs should – or even can – run the companies they found into maturity.

Fellow columnist and entrepreneur Luke Johnson says it takes at least 10 years to transform an idea from start-up to success. On that basis, Mr Stone has fallen short, despite his grandiose claim that his work on Twitter 'spanned more than half a decade'. But even for those who stay the course, the road is twisty and the destination can be a let-down.

Some entrepreneurs know they aren't cut out to run the company. In *The New New Thing*, Michael Lewis quotes Jim Clark, the man behind Silicon Graphics and Netscape: 'I can't be a venture capitalist, because I'm not that kind of person, and I can't be a manager, because I'm not that kind of person. The only thing I can do is start 'em.'

But Mr Clark is rare in his ability to move on. It is hard for parents to abandon their babies. Such entrepreneurial devotion is both a bane and a boon.

Sir Stelios Haji-Ioannou, founder of UK budget airline EasyJet, resigned as chairman in 2002 with a public acknowledgement that history was 'littered with entrepreneurs who held on to their creations for too long, failing to recognise the changing needs of the company, its business and its shareholders'. Nine years on, as a major investor in the company, he's still taking potshots at EasyJet's corporate pilots from his seat in the economy class cabin.

➡

But when a company does harness a founder's creativity, drive and bloody-minded dedication, the results can be spectacular. Mr Zuckerberg and Google's Larry Page seem set on this long-term course. Other examples include Steve Jobs at Apple, Larry Ellison at Oracle, and Bill Gates, when he led Microsoft. The phenomenon is not confined to Silicon Valley. Michael Moritz of Sequoia Capital, the US west coast venture capital firm, also cites Fred Smith at FedEx, Jeff Bezos at Amazon.com, and Rupert Murdoch at News Corp to prove that entrepreneurial zip and listed company prosperity are far from incompatible. But he adds: 'If you want to have an enduring company, it's the pursuit of a lifetime.'

One requirement is imperviousness to the temptation to make an early and possibly lucrative exit. (Mr Zuckerberg was a 20-year-old student in 2004; $10m is a lot of beer money.) Too many 'serial entrepreneurs' divide their careers into 48-month increments – in line with the vesting schedule for stock in a start-up.

A second imperative is that founders have a clear-eyed view of their strengths. Sir Richard Branson and the public markets didn't mix – he delisted Virgin Group after just two years in the 1980s – but he remains a strong public face for the brand. A generous interpretation of Mr Stone and Mr Williams' decision to step aside at Twitter is that they believe others stand a better chance of building on the microblogging service's customer success.

The risk for founders who overstay is that the eulogies of some of the business press go to their heads. If the myth of the imperial CEO can be dangerous, the myth of the visionary founder-CEO can be fatal.

Hence the final challenge, faced most acutely by Apple's Mr Jobs and his board: to identify a manager or successor with the same sense of ownership as the person who inspired the whole venture. Andy Grove, who was sufficiently talented to carry Intel's founding vision forward without looking back, is the classic example.

Twitter has now installed Dick Costolo as CEO alongside Mr Dorsey as executive chairman. But it is no disrespect to say the odds are against them as they try to sustain the company's early zest. For if there is one quest as demanding as finding an entrepreneur with a managerial bent, it is to find a manager with a true entrepreneurial gift.[127]

Source: Hill, A. (2011) The mixed blessing of a founder's devotion, *Financial Times*, 4 July 2011.
© The Financial Times Limited 2011. All Rights Reserved.

As it happens, at the time of writing, Twitter is still searching. In 2015, Mr Costolo stepped down and Mr Dorsey took over as interim chief executive.

By now, many boards would hope that science and research would help them make the right choices about succession. But the evidence is strangely mixed about how to do it, as this column, written shortly after Michael Woodford, who blew the whistle on problems at Olympus of Japan, had stepped down.

The art and science of picking a leader

By Andrew Hill

Financial Times October 24, 2011

Whatever the reason for Michael Woodford's abrupt exit from Olympus (of which more later), everyone can agree that if the board's chosen chief executive leaves prematurely, something has probably gone wrong.

It happens surprisingly frequently at large companies with heavyweight boards. Léo Apotheker lasted 11 months at Hewlett-Packard. Ian Smith – announced with a fanfare as directors' top choice to succeed Sir Crispin Davis at Reed Elsevier – stepped down in 2009 after less than nine months at the media and information company. If executives who are supposed to be the cream of the cream are souring within months of their appointment, it is a fair bet that below the top level, the incidence of fluffed hires, poor promotions and recruitment U-turns is even greater. Directors should surely be asking themselves: why are we bad at picking good leaders?

That is the title of a recent book by Jeffrey Cohn and Jay Moran, which adds to the pile of titles on the topic. The authors are consultants specialising in succession planning and executive recruitment, as are James Citrin and Julie Hembrock Daum, who wrote another recent book, *You Need a Leader – Now What?* If you look past the 'Hire us!' subtext, they offer some interesting guidelines. Interesting, but far from definitive.

Drawing on a study of CEO transition at companies in the US and Europe, Mr Citrin and Ms Hembrock Daum refine the intuition that outside hires often underperform insiders. That is largely true when outsiders are appointed to run healthy, growing companies, they say. But when a company is 'in a significantly challenged or crisis condition', the reverse is true. In the US, outside hires picked to run troubled

➡

companies are three times as likely to achieve top-quartile performance than insiders.

The snag is that the exceptions they cite punch a large hole in their broad conclusions. Anne Mulcahy, the quintessential Xerox insider, followed outsider Rick Thoman as chief executive in 2000 when the company was palpably in crisis. Mr Citrin and Ms Hembrock Daum say this 'pendulum effect' is an important exception to their overall thesis. But it is no disrespect to Ms Mulcahy, who led a successful turnround, to suggest that in Xerox's darkest hour, with investigations and bankruptcy looming, the list of external candidates must have been short. The same goes for companies that pull board members into executive positions in a crisis – the authors' second exception. Such hybrid chief executives have the best record of any type of CEO, yet boards rarely appoint them.

Matching the right individual to the right situation using the right process is complicated. However experienced, directors are people, picking people. That is always a task with unpredictable consequences – and outcomes as varied as the people involved. Knowing the essential truths of leadership selection or recognising the attributes of great leaders will help but, as Mr Cohn and Mr Moran put it, 'the trick is knowing what these attributes mean and how to spot them'. The number of books that try to teach the trick just shows how difficult it is to carry off.

When Jack Griffin lost his job as head of Time Inc this year after only five months, Jeff Bewkes, CEO of parent company Time Warner, told staff that Mr Griffin's 'leadership style and approach did not mesh' with the company's. It was a rare public reminder that appointing corporate leaders is as much art as science. If it is at all scientific, it is more like a heart transplant than a laboratory experiment. Even after a suitable replacement organ is identified, there is a risk of rejection. CEOs should have a chance to demonstrate their worth. But directors who remove a new executive who proves unsuitable – like surgeons who pick the 'wrong' heart – should probably be given greater benefit of the doubt.

I have less patience for the Olympus board, however. Mr Woodford had honed his style – identified as a reason for his dismissal – over many years at the company. He had a mandate to shake things up. Olympus directors may now feel they picked the wrong candidate. But if the ex-CEO has uncovered an unhealthy culture, ripe for reform, they may go down in history – and in the next set of headhunters' how-to manuals – as the board that picked the right man, but by mistake.[128]

FT *Source:* Hill, A. (2011) The art and science of picking a leader, *Financial Times*, 24 October 2011.
© The Financial Times Limited 2011. All Rights Reserved.

Leadership lessons:

1. Boards should monitor leaders' attitudes, not their age or their length of time in office.

2. Be careful not to overstay your welcome at the top.

3. Take the long view and do not assume that successors need to reinvent everything.

4. Family leaders almost invariably need to find professional managers to take the company on after the first generation.

5. Avoid appointing co-chief executives, which can be an excuse for indecision.

6. Succession planning is vital, but treat it as an art, rather than a science.

Chapter

9

Leading in the 21st century

When I used to write about financial markets, I would occasionally round up the year by reporting on the work of an imaginary stockbroker, Back, Track & Hindsight (and its 110-year-old head of equity analysis Nick Nostradamus), which, 'by issuing reports only after the market has moved, managed to maintain a 100 per cent record of accuracy'.

Hindsight is far easier than foresight, which is why business journalists, in particular, tend to steer clear of predictions. Innate scepticism about successes means we write a lot about failures and disasters, and somewhat less – for fear of being accused of boosterism – about successes. Perhaps affected by having covered the collapse of Enron at the turn of the century, I find I have looked back at the missteps of leaders at companies such as Nokia or Eastman Kodak more often than I have looked forward at potential successes.

What, though, does the future of leadership hold? What will leading look like in the rest of the 21st century? I see two important and interlinked influences on how leaders lead in the future: new science and new people.

New science

'Big data' has gained such ubiquity as a term that it is on the verge of becoming a useless piece of management jargon. Worse, it can be misleading, persuading bamboozled bosses that if the strategic challenge is that big, meeting it must require a big initiative, run by a big team, and backed by a big investment. In 2012, I heard from one consultant about a company that planned to spend nearly $300m over six years to 're-architect' its data. Most of that investment, he pointed out, would be wasted. By the time the six years were up, 'everything would have changed'.

Still, leaders will prosper if they use dynamic data wisely and analyse not just what happened last week, but what is happening now, using social media, the internet of things, and old-fashioned records of customer behaviour. The key will be combining data analysis with the intuition to know where it falls short. The people who can use the key will be 'rock stars', in the words of Susan Athey, a Stanford professor and economist who studies data.

Neuroscience is another discipline that is lighting up leaders' prefrontal cortex. Like all frontier science, it will be misused and mis-sold by charlatans. But at the same time, new research suggests it has the potential to change the way in which leaders work with their teams, and even to change their own flawed approaches. At Davos in 2015, neuroscientist Tania Singer presented research that shows intensive exercises in empathy, perspective-taking and mindfulness can change 'the brain's hardware'. Such exercises could make selfish leaders more 'prosocial' in their negotiations. Robert Shiller, the famous economist, appearing on the same panel in the Swiss Alps, said such findings, if confirmed (and that could still take years more verification and support) could shake the fundamental underpinnings of economics.

The third area of scientific research that will change the way leaders work is automation. When Terry Gou, founder of Foxconn, the contract manufacturer, pointed out in 2011 that within two years, he would 'employ' as many robots as workers in its China factories, I wrote that he was playing to people's worst fears 'by hinting at the replacement of awkward flesh-and-blood staff with cheap, uncomplaining machines'. At time of writing, as far as it is possible to tell, Mr Gou has not attained his goal. But in any case, the dystopian vision of managers replaced by machines, is, I think, less likely than a more optimistic future of leaders supplemented and supported by technology – a realisation of the Toyota production engineer Taiichi Ohno's idea of 'autonomation' – 'automation with a human touch' – mentioned in Chapter 3.

New people

Improvements in machine intelligence require improvements in management skills. That requirement will in turn drive leaders to look at a wider and deeper pool of candidates, changing the make-up of 'the leadership' by generation and by gender.

Stereotyping generations – old and young – seems to me unproductive, which is why I generally steer clear of using the labels (Gens X, Y and Z) applied by others. I also believe it is possible that some of the characteristics attributed to younger generations – 'irreverent, change-seeking, challenging, better informed, mobile, and connected', as Moisés Naím has described the under-30s[129] – may fade as they get older.

Even so, the anecdotal and empirical evidence of a gulf in attitudes between generations of management is strong. Sir Ian Cheshire, when chief executive of Kingfisher, the UK-based home improvement group, conducted internal research showing that of the group's top 300 managers, executives aged over 35 tended to hoard their accumulated knowledge, while younger managers were happier to share it.

The sharing has to go both ways. Stefan Sommer, chief executive of ZF Friedrichshafen, the German car parts manufacturer, has called the under-30s the 'Feedback Generation'. Speaking on a panel I chaired in 2014, he said that in the past, 'no grumbling was praise enough' for an employee. But now his younger staff 'like the "like" button'. Above all, leaders have to stop offering young workers what London Business School's Lynda Gratton has called 'crap-awful work'.

As current leaders improve their dialogue with this younger generation, the diversity of leadership will also, by necessity, change. It is about time. While the symbolic power of campaigns to introduce more women and ethnic minorities onto listed company boards is not in doubt, the real pressure needs to come further down the pipeline, in advancing a different-looking and, crucially, different-*thinking* group into executive positions.

Research has shown how more cognitively diverse teams are more innovative. But they are also less homogeneous and less harmonious – which makes such teams more difficult to lead and manage. In a further complication, as I have suggested earlier, future leaders will be running teams that are looser, less committed, more spread out, than their counterparts today. In the words of one experienced chief executive, business leaders are already 'taking care of the connections [in the network] more than the nodes'. Their successors will have to raise their game further and improve their own skills, to make the most of the new science and the new people that fuel the networked teams of the future.

How soon will this happen? Prediction really is futile in this case. But I do not necessarily think the pace of the change will be or needs to be as rapid as some revolutionary thinkers believe. Here is what I wrote in 2014, in a companion piece to the column that appeared in this book's introduction.

Radical change that starts with small steps at big companies

By Andrew Hill

Financial Times November 17, 2014

Gary Hamel still talks and writes with the passion of a revolutionary. In a recent blogpost, the management writer played with his own theory of the 'core competencies' of companies, conceived with the late CK Prahalad, by pointing out their core incompetencies of inertia, incrementalism and insipidity.[130]

Last week, I listened to him telling the Global Peter Drucker Forum that the corporate bureaucracy plaguing companies such as Delta Air Lines, Tesco, Samsung and Salesforce.com must be 'put to death'. Managers need to shed vestigial beliefs handed down by 'long-dead CEOs, ego-polishing consultants and dry scholars', he said.

Stirring stuff. But while there is plenty of idealism on tap at gatherings of management thinkers, it increasingly comes with a refreshing chaser of realism.

It is no disrespect to idealists and firebrands to point out that an 'Arab spring' of populist management reform is unlikely. At large companies, incremental change may be one of the best ways to achieve a radical transformation. Speaking in Vienna, birthplace of management thinker Peter Drucker, Professor Hamel said change should not come only from small greenfield start-ups; their older, larger 'brownfield' cousins also need to find a new way of managing.

One prerequisite, as I said in my last column, is that companies should stop appointing 'default managers', who are content merely to fit in with the old framework. 'Organisations are hiring great people and turning them into average performers – and they're doing it very, very fast,' warned Bill Fischer of IMD business school. Another is to stop assuming that change in corporate structure – say, from publicly listed companies, to employee ownership – will automatically put an end to mismanagement or reignite innovation. It is more important to ensure there is no dominant monoculture of one corporate form.

'Brownfield' corporate leaders also need to see, and even experience, new models of organisations similar to their own that are successfully changing management systems. However, favourite examples of flat-hierarchy or super-transparent companies such as Ricardo Semler's Semco, the Brazilian engineering group, WL Gore, US manufacturer of Gore-Tex fabric, or Morning Star, the self-managing Californian tomato processor, are in danger of overuse.

In any case, it is hard to convince a conventional manager that peer-based pay and mutual 'understandings' between colleagues, which replace conventional compensation policies and contracts at Morning Star, could transfer to a traditional organisation.

Examples cited in Vienna could expand the canon of management innovation a little. Professor Fischer has been studying DSM, a Dutch coalminer that has turned itself into a life sciences and materials science group.[131] It has overcome the blight of centralisation that often afflicts innovation projects by running them in parallel – what it calls a 'bowling alley' approach – on a platform that allows innovators a greater say in how innovation as a whole is pursued. Haier of China, already something of a pioneer in the use of self-organising units that compete internally for opportunities, has spun off its logistics arm – 'de-Haierising' itself, in Prof Fischer's words – so it can offer its China-wide expertise to competitors.

The next step must be to take such cases out of the classroom and present the practical advantages to interested companies. Steve Denning, the veteran management writer, is launching a 'learning consortium' of such organisations.[132] Members arrange site visits to highlight to the others the practical benefits and risks of applying emerging management practices.

Contradictions will have to be overcome: Salesforce, which Prof Hamel castigates as a bureaucratic monster, is an exemplar of 'agile' management for Mr Denning. Some paradoxes must be embraced: Prof Fischer points out, for instance, that only 'self-assured, courageous, top-down leaders' will be comfortable enough to liberate people to develop new ideas and change management practice. These are the same leaders that sometimes balk at abandoning the power they have built up.

But by opening up and testing new ideas from across their companies and beyond, far-sighted leaders could achieve a more radical transformation than they ever anticipated – even if it starts with small steps.[133]

Source: Hill, A. (2014) Radical change that starts with small steps at big companies, *Financial Times*, 17 November 2014.
© The Financial Times Limited 2014. All Rights Reserved.

In this book I have tried to summarise the eight 'acts' that leaders need to master in their day-to-day efforts to keep their heads above water long enough to shout some encouragement and instructions to their teams.

I am under no illusion about the difficulty of doing this. In 2013, I interviewed the greatest sceptic about leadership and management of them all – Scott Adams, the creator of the Dilbert cartoon strip. He had just published a mordant book, based on his own experience and called *How to Fail at Almost Everything and Still Win Big*. He said *How to Fail* was neither a self-help book nor a book of advice – though to my mind it was obviously both of those things – deriding the genres as 'generally worthless'. 'You've got a million monkeys doing a million things and some of them are going to succeed,' he said. 'When they do they're going to say: "Right before I had that big success I was scratching my ass, so let's write a book about how everybody should scratch their ass because [it] works for me."'

A running joke of the Dilbert cartoons is the incompetence of leaders, an extension of the 'Dilbert principle' that 'the most ineffective workers will be systematically moved to the place where they can do the least damage – management'. Asked to identify the business leader he most admired, I half expected him to condemn them all. Instead, he picked Bill Gates of Microsoft, because, he explained – with no hint of the cynicism that drives his comic strip – 'starting Microsoft was the small part of his life [and] the big part's still ahead: the things that are really going to change civilisation'.

Leaders will continue to have to lead in the headlines. Many will stumble. Their job will if anything get harder and more complex in the coming decades. Most will have times when, like John Mackey of Whole Foods, quoted at the start of this book, they are hailed as visionaries, and condemned as village idiots. But a few will succeed in hitting the headlines for the right reasons.

What did you think of this book?

We're really keen to hear from you about this book, so that we can make our publishing even better.

Please log on to the following website and leave us your feedback.

It will only take a few minutes and your thoughts are invaluable to us.

www.pearsoned.co.uk/bookfeedback

Bibliography

Introduction:

Green, S. (2009) *Good Value: Reflections on Money, Morality and an Uncertain World*. London: Allen Lane.

Ibarra, H. (2015) *Act Like a Leader, Think Like a Leader*. Boston: Harvard Business Review Press.

March, J. and **Weil, T.** (2005) *On Leadership: A Short Course*. Oxford: John Wiley & Sons.

Chapter 1. Planning

McGrath, R.G. (2013) *The End of Competitive Advantage: How to Keep Your Strategy Moving as Fast as Your Business*. Boston:Harvard Business Review Press.

McKinney, D. (2012) *The Commando Way: Extraordinary Business Execution*. London: Lid Publishing.

Porter, M. (1985) *Competitive Advantage: Creating and Sustaining Superior Performance*. London: Collier Macmillan.

Rumelt, R. (2011) *Good Strategy/Bad Strategy: The Difference and Why It Matters*. New York: Crown Business.

Style, C., **Beale, N.** and **Ellery, D.**, (eds) (2012) *In Business and Battle: Strategic Leadership in the Civilian and Military Spheres*. Farnham and Burlington, VT: Gower.

Taleb, N.N. (2007) *The Black Swan: The Impact of the Highly Improbable*. New York: Random House.

Warren, K. (2012) *The Trouble with Strategy*. Princes Risborough, Buckinghamshire: Strategy Dynamics Ltd.

Chapter 2. Moving

Amabile, **T**. and **Kramer**, **S**. (2011) *The Progress Principle: Using Small Wins to Ignite Joy, Engagement, and Creativity at Work*. Boston: Harvard Business Review Press.

Goffee, **R**. and **Jones**, **G**. (2006) *Why Should Anyone be Led by You? What It Takes to Be an Authentic Leader*. Boston: Harvard Business School Press.

Sloan, **A.P**. (1964) *My Years With General Motors*. Garden City, NY: Doubleday.

Chapter 3. Making

Anthony, **S**. (2104) *The First Mile: A Launch Manual for Getting Great Ideas to the Market*. Boston: Harvard Business Review Press.

Chan Kim, **W**. and **Mauborgne**, **R**. (2005) *Blue Ocean Strategy: How to Create Uncontested Market Space and Make the Competition Irrelevant*. Boston, MA: Harvard Business Review Press.

Delves Broughton, **P**. (2013) *Life's a Pitch: What the World's Best Salespeople Can Teach Us All*. London: Portfolio Penguin.

Dyer, **J**., **Gregersen**, **H**. and **Christensen**, **C**. (2011) *The Innovator's DNA: Mastering the Five Skills of Disruptive Innovators*. Boston: Harvard Business Review Press.

Liker, **J**. (2004) *The Toyota Way: 14 Management Principles from the World's Greatest Manufacturer*. New York: McGraw-Hill Education.

Marsh, **P**. (2012) *The New Industrial Revolution: Consumers, Globalization and the End of Mass Production*. New Haven: Yale University Press.

Pink, **D**. (2012) *To Sell Is Human: The Surprising Truth about Moving Others*. New York: Riverhead Books.

Vogelstein, **F**. (2013) *Battle of the Titans: How the Fight to the Death between Apple and Google is Transforming our Lives*. London: William Collins.

Chapter 4. Shaping

Collins, **J**. and **Porras**, **J**. (1994) *Built to Last: Successful Habits of Visionary Companies*. New York: HarperBusiness.

de Rond, M. (2012) *There Is an I in Team: What Elite Athletes and Coaches Really Know About High Performance*. Boston: Harvard Business Review Press.

Geneen, H., with **Moscow, A.** (1984) Managing. Garden City, NY: Doubleday.

Khanna, T. and **Palepu, K.** (2010) *Winning in Emerging Markets*. Boston: Harvard Business Press.

Micklethwait, J. and **Wooldridge, A.** (2003) *The Company: A Short History of a Revolutionary Idea*. New York: Modern Library.

Chapter 5. Growing

Conyers, Y. and **Qiao, G.** (2014) *The Lenovo Way: Managing a Diverse Global Company for Optimal Performance*. New York: McGraw-Hill Education.

Dahlvig, A. (2012) *The Ikea Edge: Building Global Growth and Social Good at the World's Most Iconic Home Store*. New York: McGraw-Hill.

Fisman, R. and **Sullivan, T.** (2013) *The Org: The Underlying Logic of the Office*. New York: Twelve.

Quelch, J. and **Jocz, K.** (2012) *All Business is Local: Why Place Matters More than Ever in a Global, Virtual World*. New York: Portfolio Penguin.

Smit, H. and **Moraitis, T.** (2015) *Playing at Acquisitions: Behavioral Option Games*. Princeton: Princeton University Press.

Chapter 6. Coping

McLean, B. and **Nocera, J.** (2010) *All the Devils Are Here: The Hidden History of the Financial Crisis*. New York: Portfolio Penguin.

Ward, C. (2011) *And the Band Played On: The Enthralling Account of What Happened After the Titanic Sank*. London: Hodder & Stoughton.

Wilson, F. (2011) *How To Survive the Titanic: The Sinking of J Bruce Ismay*. New York: HarperCollins.

Chapter 7. Sharing

Drucker, P. (1990) *Managing the Non-Profit Organization: Practices and Principles*. New York: HarperCollins.

Haque, U. (2011) *The New Capitalist Manifesto: Building a Disruptively Better Business.* Boston: Harvard Business Press.

Martin, R. (2011) *Fixing the Game: Bubbles, Crashes and What Capitalism Can Learn from the NFL.* Boston: Harvard Business School Publishing.

Moss Kanter, R. (2009) *SuperCorp: How Vanguard Companies Create Innovation, Profits, Growth and Social Good.* New York: Crown Business.

Nayar, V. (2010) *Employees First, Customers Second: Turning Conventional Management Upside Down.* Boston: Harvard Business Press.

Robertson, B. (2015) *Holacracy: The New Management System that Redefines Management.* New York: Henry Holt and Company.

Chapter 8. Leaving

Citrin, J. and **Hembrock Daum, J.** (2011) *You Need a Leader – Now What? How to Choose the Best Person for your Organization.* New York: Crown Business.

Cohn, J. and **Moran, J.** (2011) *Why Are We Bad at Picking Good Leaders? A Better Way to Evaluate Leadership Potential.* San Francisco: Jossey-Bass.

Frisch, B. (2012) *Who's in the Room? How Great Leaders Structure and Manage the Teams Around Them.* San Francisco: Jossey-Bass.

Hensmans, M., Johnson, G. and **Yip , G.** (2013) *Strategic Transformation: Changing While Winning.* Basingstoke, Hampshire and New York: Palgrave Macmillan.

Lewis, M. (2000) *The New New Thing: A Silicon Valley Story.* New York: W.W. Norton.

Chapter 9. Leading in the 21st Century

Adams, S. (2013) *How to Fail at Almost Everything and Still Win Big: Kind of the Story of My Life.* New York: Portfolio Penguin.

Naím, M. (2013) *The End of Power: From Boardrooms to Battlefields and Churches to States, Why Being in Charge Isn't What it Used to Be.* New York: Basic Books.

Notes

1 'The Monday interview: John Mackey' **www.ft.com/cms/s/2/ ab2996e0-da9f-11e2-a237-00144feab7de.html**

2 *On Leadership*, by James March and Thierry Weil **http://books. google.co.uk/books?id=th5vFtgPHi8C&pg=PA97&source=gbs_ toc_r&cad=4#v=one page&q&f=false**

3 **www.newstatesman.com/culture/2014/10/ grayson-perry-rise-and-fall-default-man**

4 'Rebalancing society' **www.mintzberg.org/sites/default/files/ rebalancing_society_pamphlet.pdf**

5 'Forget Mozart, companies now prefer a steady Salieri as CEO' **www. ft.com/cms/s/0/760e6d80-6123-11e4-b935-00144feabdc0.html**

6 'Better management could spur a new era of economic growth', HBR blogs **https://hbr.org/2014/05/ better-management-could-spur-a-new-era-of-economic-growth/**

7 'The default mode for managers needs a reset' **www.ft.com/cms/s/0/ a8fe78a8-65e6-11e4-898f-00144feabdc0.html**

8 *Act Like a Leader, Think Like a Leader* by Herminia Ibarra.

9 'Managing to lead', Henry Mintzberg **www.mintzberg.org/blog/ to-lead**

10 'Strategies founder on fluff and buzzwords' **www.ft.com/cms/ s/0/5c6712b2-95e6-11e0-ba20-00144feab49a.html**

11 'Business lessons from the front line' **www.ft.com/cms/ s/0/96963fdc-0e2e-11e2-8d92-00144feabdc0.html**

12 'An academic who shares his values' **www.ft.com/cms/s/0/5a62e6d0- e046-11e0-ba12-00144feabdc0.html**

13 'Banking is heading towards its Spotify moment' **www.ft.com/ cms/s/0/e1ae654a-c791-11e2-9c52-00144feab7de.html**

14 'Perpetual pilots are the new goal for strategy' **www.ft.com/cms/s/0/ ebf7cb8a-da84-11e2-a237-00144feab7de.html**

15 'Look into the future before it is too late' **www.ft.com/cms/ s/0/28a76d1a-95e9-11e1-9d9d-00144feab49a.html**

16 Kim Warren, who has taught strategic management at London Business School, fired back in his book *The Trouble with Strategy*, claiming that I had produced a 'trivial and ill-informed dismissal of the whole idea of strategy' – which was not quite how I saw it.

17 'It's time to make management a true profession', HBR blogs https://hbr.org/2008/10/its-time-to-make-management-a-true-profession/ar/1

18 'Experience trumps exams for strategists' www.ft.com/cms/s/0/b95ef8ce-6c2b-11e1-b00f-00144feab49a.html

19 RiskMap, Control Risks https://riskmap.controlrisks.com/

20 In August 2015, as a direct consequence of the impact of that Budget, Partnership Assurance and Just Retirement announced they would combine to form a new company, to be called JRP.

21 'When a haven harbours unseen risk' www.ft.com/cms/s/0/bca61292-b0f8-11e3-9f6f-00144feab7de.html

22 'Globalization's critical imbalances' www.mckinsey.com/insights/globalization/globalizations_critical_imbalances

23 'Three cheers for New Year trepidation' www.ft.com/cms/s/0/c3ca5540-2718-11e1-b9ec-00144feabdc0.html

24 'Bosses are blinded by their bonus obsession' www.ft.com/cms/s/0/e269b47c-32eb-11e0-9a61-00144feabdc0.html

25 'Building your company's vision' HBR blogs https://hbr.org/1996/09/building-your-companys-vision/ar/1

26 'Tiny bursts of joy pave the way to BHAGs' www.ft.com/cms/s/0/afcc6468-dd33-11e0-b4f2-00144feabdc0.html

27 'We should stop trying to change the world' www.ft.com/cms/s/0/b7d98ebc-74f3-11e1-ab8b-00144feab49a.html

28 www.vanityfair.com/news/2012/07/microsoft-downfall-emails-steve-ballmer

29 'Forced ranking is a relic of an HR tool' www.ft.com/cms/s/0/0243818e-cd09-11e1-92c1-00144feabdc0.html

30 'Inside Amazon: wrestling big ideas in a bruising workplace' www.nytimes.com/2015/08/16/technology/inside-amazon-wrestling-big-ideas-in-a-bruising-workplace.html

31 'Gratitude as moral sentiment', by De Steno *et al.* www.ncbi.nlm.nih.gov/pubmed/20364907

32 'A little thanks goes a long way', by Grant and Gino http://psycnet.apa.org/journals/psp/98/6/946/

33 'Thank you can be the hardest words' www.ft.com/cms/s/0/855ddfd2-34a2-11e2-8b86-00144feabdc0.html

34 'Corporate values and employee cynicism', Harvard Business School http://hbswk.hbs.edu/item/5229.html

35 '"Purpose" is the preachy new CEO buzzword' www.ft.com/cms/
s/0/4acea19e-82c6-11e3-9d7e-00144feab7de.html

36 'A funny thing happened on the way to the bottom line' http://amj.
aom.org/content/42/2/219.abstract

37 'Bosses in drag can set a good tone at the top' www.ft.com/cms/
s/0/26ad634a-7f88-11e3-94d2-00144feabdc0.html

38 'How P&G tripled its innovation success rate' HBR blogs
https://hbr.org/2011/06/how-pg-tripled-its-innovation-success-
rate/ar/1

39 'The tight controls needed for creativity' www.ft.com/cms/
s/0/18989672-8b01-11e0-b2f1-00144feab49a.html

40 Prof Nakamura shared the Nobel Prize for Physics in 2014 for his work.

41 'Stealing fire: creative deviance in the evolution of new ideas', by
Charalampos Mainemelis http://amr.aom.org/content/35/4/558.
short

42 State of Create Study, Adobe www.adobe.com/aboutadobe/
pressroom/pdfs/Adobe_State_of_Create_Global_Benchmark_
Study.pdf

43 'Understanding the race for impact' http://futurestep.com/insights/
understanding-the-race-for-impact/

44 'How to conform to creative deviance' www.ft.com/cms/
s/0/892566c2-9082-11e1-9e2e-00144feab49a.html

45 'The rules of innovation can be flexible' www.ft.com/cms/s/0/
f6b686a6-453c-11e3-997c-00144feabdc0.html

46 'Nokia's bad call on smartphones', Wall Street Journal www.wsj.com/
articles/SB10001424052702304388004577531002591315494

47 'The day Google had to "start over" on Android', The Atlantic
www.theatlantic.com/technology/archive/2013/12/
the-day-google-had-to-start-over-on-android/282479/

48 'Inside the fall of BlackBerry: how the smartphone inventor failed
to adapt', The Globe and Mail www.theglobeandmail.com/report-
on-business/the-inside-story-of-why-blackberry-is-failing/
article14563602/?page=all

49 'Apple Watch shows the strategic ripple effects of a big splash' www.
ft.com/cms/s/0/49d96f4e-c8d4-11e4-b43b-00144feab7de.html

50 'Guru: Taiichi Ohno', The Economist www.economist.com/
node/13941150

51 'Toyoda's legacy goes well beyond the lean' www.ft.com/cms/s/0/
aa2759f8-26c6-11e3-9dc0-00144feab7de.html

52 'Portrait of a perfect salesman' www.ft.com/cms/s/0/c622c20c-943f-
11e1-bb0d-00144feab49a.html

53 'The web has not yet killed the art of sales' www.ft.com/cms/
s/0/422c8180-55be-11e3-b6e7-00144feabdc0.html

54 Clarence Birdseye, Wikipedia **http://en.wikipedia.org/wiki/ Clarence_Birdseye**

55 'Contortions are required for Cirque du Soleil to keep its magic' **www. ft.com/cms/s/0/581f73a2-e9d4-11e4-ae1c-00144feab7de.html**

56 'Skilled workers shortfall of 40m forecast' **www.ft.com/cms/ s/0/13e0ae56-316f-11e2-b68b-00144feabdc0.html**

57 'Introducing T-shaped managers: knowledge management's next generation', HBR blogs **http://hbr.org/2001/03/introducing-t-shaped-managers-knowledge-managements-next-generation/ ar/1**

58 'An all-rounder may not be the right fit' **www.ft.com/cms/ s/0/276f1076-397f-11e2-8881-00144feabdc0.html**

59 'Why teams don't work', HBR blogs **https://hbr.org/2009/05/ why-teams-dont-work/ar/1**

60 'The diminishing returns of all-star team', *Strategy + Business*, **www. strategy-business.com/article/re00112?gko=018a4**

61 The 'Pietersen issue' resurfaced in 2015, when England declined to select the in-form cricketer. A young England team went on to record a resounding and unexpected victory over Australia.

62 'The right number of stars for a team' **www.ft.com/cms/ s/0/4d958524-e6fe-11e1-8a74-00144feab49a.html**

63 'Thomson Reuters chief looks to next phase' **www.ft.com/cms/s/0/ dea8623e-7026-11e0-bea7-00144feabdc0.html**

64 For example, 'Reinventing the firm', a 2009 paper from Demos **www. demos.co.uk/files/Reinventing_the_firm.pdf?1252652788**

65 'It's the managers, not the model' **www.ft.com/cms/s/0/6b8db826-7a80-11e0-8762-00144feabdc0.html**

66 'Road tests favour employee-ownership model' **www.ft.com/cms/s/0/ fe8aa766-7c23-11e0-a386-00144feabdc0.html#axzz3qK0WCUNj**
There was also a further interesting coda to that exchange: in 2015, Tullis Russell, a paper mill Mr Erdal's family had sold to its employees in 1994, went out of business. In that case, neither management nor model was to blame. 'No ownership system can save a business that is undermined by global competition,' Mr Erdal commented.

67 'Killing projects is the hardest innovation' **www.ft.com/cms/s/0/ c313c96a-965c-11e2-9ab2-00144feabdc0.html**

68 'Breaking up is not a sign of failure' **www.ft.com/cms/s/0/ef29d5d8-2806-11e0-8abc-00144feab49a.html**

69 'The impact of culture on the management values and beliefs of Korean firms', by Young Hack Song and Christopher Meek **www.freepatentsonline.com/article/Journal-Comparative-International-Management/78738324.html**

70 'You can take the cult out of culture' www.ft.com/cms/s/0/ca02a376-f2ac-11e1-86e0-00144feabdc0.html

71 'The first 90 days in a new job', Mary Barra www.linkedin.com/pulse/first-90-days-new-job-mary-barra

72 'Who will train the new generation of plug and play workers?' www.ft.com/cms/s/0/c871a72a-a4c3-11e4-b943-00144feab7de.html

73 'How Drucker thought about complexity', HBR blogs https://hbr.org/2013/06/how-drucker-thought-about-comp

74 'The nature of the firm' by R.H. Coase www.jstor.org/stable/2626876?seq=1#page_scan_tab_contents

75 'The institutional structure of production' www.nobelprize.org/nobel_prizes/economic-sciences/laureates/1991/coase-lecture.html

76 'New life in the idea of the big company' www.ft.com/cms/s/0/bca97630-1634-11e3-856f-00144feabdc0.html

77 Speech to Melbourne Mining Club, London, by Mick Davis, chief executive, Xstrata, June 2009.

78 'Playing at serial acquisitions', by Han Smit and Thras Moraitis, *California Management Review*, Fall 2010 www.jstor.org/stable/10.1525/cmr.2010.53.1.56?seq=1#page_scan_tab_contents Smit and Moraitis published a book about their theories in 2015, *Playing at Acquisitions: Behavioral Option Games* (Princeton University Press).

79 'Chance encounters of the M&A' kind www.ft.com/cms/s/0/2485abda-06e6-11e1-90de-00144feabdc0.html

80 'Corporate marriages often end in divorce' www.ft.com/cms/s/0/2d8bd966-b6f5-11e0-a8b8-00144feabdc0.html

81 'Speed of execution in leadership shake-ups is the secret to M&A success', Cass Business School www.cass.city.ac.uk/__data/assets/pdf_file/0015/213324/Successful-Dealmaking_Final.pdf

82 'What Lenovo can teach us about making takeovers work' www.ft.com/cms/s/0/c9148648-55e5-11e4-a3c9-00144feab7de.html

83 'How not to stifle your new subsidiary' www.ft.com/cms/s/0/c2d9280c-a1f4-11e2-8971-00144feabdc0.html

84 'Wanted: marketers who know their place' www.ft.com/cms/s/0/9497b348-435c-11e1-9f28-00144feab49a.html

85 'Built to become: corporate longevity and strategic leadership', by Robert Burgelman www.gsb.stanford.edu/faculty-research/working-papers/built-become-corporate-longevity-strategic-leadership

86 'Yamaha's third attempt at cars will be worth the detour' www.ft.com/cms/s/0/a6aba2fa-ce47-11e4-86fc-00144feab7de.html

87 'The CEO report', Heidrick & Struggles/Oxford Saïd Business School **www.heidrick.com/Knowledge-Center/Publication/ The-CEO-Report**

88 'Self-doubt in snow boots: the reality of Davos for most CEOs' **www. ft.com/cms/s/0/3dd892d0-9cc2-11e4-971b-00144feabdc0.html**

89 'My grandfather, the Titanic's violinist', *The Spectator* **www.spectator. co.uk/features/7141073/my-grandfather-the-titanics-violinist/**

90 'We're sunk if bosses are first in the lifeboat' **www.ft.com/cms/s/0/ f09bd768-ccf2-11e0-88fe-00144feabdc0.html?siteedition=uk**

91 'How the other Fukushima plant survived', HBR blog **https://hbr. org/2014/07/how-the-other-fukushima-plant-survived/ar/1**

92 'The collapse of sensemaking in organizations' **www.nifc.gov/ safety/mann_gulch/suggested_reading/The_Collapse_of_ Sensemaking_in_Organizations_The_Mann_Gulch.pdf**

93 'Cool heads improvise in crisis and calm' **www.ft.com/ cms/s/0/195e0058-081f-11e4-9afc-00144feab7de.html**

94 'The buck stops both at chairs and chiefs' **www.ft.com/cms/s/0/ ff23e2f4-c426-11e1-9c1e-00144feabdc0.html**

95 'Wealth shocks and executive compensation: evidence from CEO divorce' **http://papers.ssrn.com/sol3/papers. cfm?abstract_id=2140668**

96 'Personal life is not off limits for the board' **www.ft.com/cms/ s/0/898b1d6a-d284-11e2-aac2-00144feab7de.html**

97 'Why must financiers meditate in secret?' **www.ft.com/cms/s/0/ ef9b7d86-cc5f-11e3-bd33-00144feabdc0.html**

98 'Ex-Enron CEO Skilling defends his role in fall' **www.chron.com/ business/enron/article/Ex-Enron-CEO-Skilling-defends-his-role- in-fall-2075180.php**

99 'Self-delusion will sink Sepp Blatter just as it sank Dick Fuld' **www. ft.com/cms/s/0/6a34a232-05eb-11e5-b676-00144feabdc0.html**

100 'End of the imperial corporate leader' **www.ft.com/cms/ s/0/735bd948-4ac6-11e3-ac3d-00144feabdc0.html**

101 'Flags of inconvenience', *The Economist* **www.economist.com/news/ business/21602237-flags-inconvenience**

102 'Corporate citizens of the world owe fealty to us all' **www.ft.com/ cms/s/0/56cf88ae-e695-11e3-b8c7-00144feabdc0.html**

103 'Zappos and the collapse of corporate hierarchies' **www.ft.com/ cms/s/0/f3377dba-73a8-11e3-beeb-00144feabdc0.html**

104 Internal memo, reported by Quartz **http://qz.com/370616/internal- memo-zappos-is-offering-severance-to-employees-who-arent-all- in-with-holacracy/**

105 Etsy S-1 filing **www.sec.gov/Archives/edgar/ data/1370637/000119312515077045/d806992ds1.html**

106 'Technology at work: the future of innovation and employment'
www.oxfordmartin.ox.ac.uk/publications/view/1883

107 'Why I hope Etsy survives flotation with its soul intact' www.ft.com/
cms/s/0/4eb29b92-c3ea-11e4-a02e-00144feab7de.html

108 'What are the barriers to volunteering?' NCVO http://data.ncvo.org.
uk/a/almanac14/what-are-the-barriers-to-volunteering/

109 World Giving Index 2014 www.cafonline.org/about-us/
publications/2014-publications/world-giving-index-2014

110 'What business can learn from the voluntary sector',
NCVO http://blogs.ncvo.org.uk/2014/09/10/
what-business-can-learn-from-the-voluntary-sector/

111 'The volunteer spirit that binds a team more than cash' www.ft.com/
cms/s/0/1a7e7bfa-9746-11e4-9636-00144feabdc0.html

112 'A bit of selfishness is all to the social good' www.ft.com/cms/
s/0/9be5fe44-7f10-11e1-a06e-00144feab49a.html

113 'Creating shared value', HBR blog https://hbr.org/2011/01/
the-big-idea-creating-shared-value/ar/1

114 'Society and the right kind of capitalism' www.ft.com/cms/
s/0/7fb25830-3de9-11e0-99ac-00144feabdc0.html

115 'CEO succession 2010', Booz & Co (now Strategy&) www.
strategyand.pwc.com/uk/home/press_contacts/displays/
CEO_Succession_2010_article

116 Walter Zable died in June 2012, aged 97.

117 'No more heroes: the future of leadership and management in the
NHS', The King's Fund www.kingsfund.org.uk/publications/
future-leadership-and-management-nhs

118 'All I am saying is give CEOs a chance' www.ft.com/cms/
s/0/6725c48c-8565-11e0-ae32-00144feabdc0.html

119 'The best performing CEOs in the world', HBR blog https://hbr.
org/2013/01/the-best-performing-ceos-in-the-world

120 'S&P 500 CEO transitions', Spencer Stuart www.spencerstuart.
com/~/media/pdf%20files/research%20and%20insight%20pdfs/
sp500ceotransition2014finalb25feb2015.pdf?la=en

121 'A stepping stone links Tesco's Philip Clarke and Man Utd's Moyes'
www.ft.com/cms/s/0/cc78fb04-10b0-11e4-812b-00144feabdc0.
html

122 'Tata can take a long view on succession' www.ft.com/cms/s/0/
a04030ce-1762-11e1-b00e-00144feabdc0.html

123 'Inside the family firm: The role of families in succession decisions
and performance' www.nber.org/papers/w12356

124 'Tony Benn 1925–2014', *The Spectator* http://blogs.new.spectator.
co.uk/2014/03/tony-benn-1925-2014-a-politician-who-actually-
believes-in-people/

125 'A patriarch Murdoch should have emulated' **www.ft.com/cms/ s/0/2e00feee-b5d5-11e3-b40e-00144feabdc0.html**

126 'More than two reasons against dual heads' **www.ft.com/cms/s/0/ ba94ef96-482c-11e1-b1b4-00144feabdc0.html**

127 'The mixed blessing of a founder's devotion' **www.ft.com/cms/ s/0/3069a7ac-a666-11e0-ae9c-00144feabdc0.html**

128 'The art and science of picking a leader' **www.ft.com/cms/s/0/ a0b59f66-fbca-11e0-9283-00144feab49a.html**

129 *The End of Power*, by Moisés Naím.

130 'The core incompetencies of the corporation', HBR blogs **https://hbr. org/2014/10/the-core-incompetencies-of-the-corporation/**

131 'Unlock employee innovation that fits with your strategy' HBR blogs **https://hbr.org/2014/10/ unlock-employee-innovation-that-fits-with-your-strategy/**

132 Learning Consortium, Scrum Alliance **www.scrumalliance.org/ why-scrum/learning-consortium**

133 'Radical change that starts with small steps at big companies' **www. ft.com/cms/s/0/ad47a4d6-6e40-11e4-afe5-00144feabdc0.html**

Index